DIY Project Based
ELA and History

Are you interested in using Project Based Learning to revamp your lessons, but aren't sure how to get started? In *DIY Project Based Learning for ELA and History*, award-winning teacher and Edutopia blogger Heather Wolpert-Gawron makes it fun and easy! Project Based Learning (PBL) encourages students and teachers alike to abandon their dusty textbooks, and instead embrace a form of curriculum design focused on student engagement, innovation, and creative problem-solving. A leading name in this field, Heather Wolpert-Gawron shares some of her most popular units for ELA and History in this exciting new collection. This book is an essential resource for teachers looking to:

- create their own Project Based Learning units;
- engage students in their education by grounding lessons in real-world problems and encouraging them to develop creative solutions;
- incorporate role-playing into everyday learning;
- develop real-world lessons to get students to understand the life-long relevance of what they are learning;
- assess multiple skills and subject areas in an integrated way;
- collaborate with teachers across subject areas;
- test authentic skills and set authentic goals for their students to grow as individuals.

Part I of the book features six full units, complete with student samples, targeted rubrics, a checklist to keep students on track, and even "Homework Hints." Part II is a mix-and-match section of tools you can use to create your own PBL-aligned lessons. The tools are available as eResources on our website, www.routledge.com/9781138891623, so you can print and use them in your classroom immediately.

Heather Wolpert-Gawron is an award-winning middle school teacher and a popular blogger through Tweenteacher.com and Edutopia.org. She has authored two other books with Routledge Eye On Education.

Other Eye On Education Books
Available from Routledge

(www.routledge.com/eyeoneducation)

DIY Project Based Learning for Math and Science
Heather Wolpert-Gawron

Writing Behind Every Door: Teaching Common Core Writing in the Content Areas
Heather Wolpert-Gawron

'Tween Crayons and Curfews: Tips for Middle School Teachers
Heather Wolpert-Gawron

Rebuilding Research Writing: Strategies for Sparking Informational Inquiry
Nanci Werner-Burke, Karin Knaus, and Amy Helt DeCamp

Beyond the Classroom: Collaborating with Colleagues and Parents to Build Core Literacy
Nanci Werner-Burke, Editor

Big Skills for the Common Core: Literacy Strategies for the 6–12 Classroom
Amy Benjamin and Michael Hugelmeyer

Teaching the Common Core Speaking and Listening Standards: Strategies and Digital Tools
Kristen Swanson

The Common Core Grammar Toolkit: Using Mentor Texts to Teach the Language Standards in Grades 6–8
Sean Ruday

Authentic Learning Experiences: A Real-World Approach to Project-Based Learning
Dayna Laur

Vocabulary Strategies That Work: Do This—Not That!
Lori G. Wilfong

Nonfiction Strategies That Work: Do This—Not That!
Lori G. Wilfong

Writing Strategies That Work: Do This—Not That!
Lori G. Wilfong

Common Core Reading Lessons: Pairing Literary and Nonfiction Texts to Promote Deeper Understanding
Stacey O'Reilly and Angie Stooksbury

DIY Project Based Learning for ELA and History

Heather Wolpert-Gawron

Routledge
Taylor & Francis Group

NEW YORK AND LONDON

First published 2016
by Routledge
711 Third Avenue, New York, NY 10017

and by Routledge
2 Park Square, Milton Park, Abingdon, Oxon, OX14 4RN

Routledge is an imprint of the Taylor & Francis Group, an informa business

Library of Congress Cataloging-in-Publication Data
Wolpert-Gawron, Heather.
  DIY project-based learning in ELA and history / by Heather
Wolpert-Gawron.
    pages cm
  Includes bibliographical references.
  1. Project method in teaching. 2. Language arts (Middle school)
  3. Active learning. 4. History—Study and teaching (Middle school)
  I. Title.
  LB1027.43.W65 2015
  371.3'6—dc23
                                                    2014049610

ISBN: 978-1-138-89161-6 (hbk)
ISBN: 978-1-138-89162-3 (pbk)
ISBN: 978-1-315-70958-1 (ebk)

Typeset in Palatino
by RefineCatch Limited, Bungay, Suffolk, UK

To Benjamin and Samwise,
If Project Based Learning is about the journey through which we learn,
then being your mom is the best adventure ever.

Contents

eResources

The Mix and Match Lesson materials in the book are also available as free eResources on our website so you can easily print and copy them for classroom use.

Go to the book's product page (www.routledge.com/9781138891623), and then click on the tab that says eResources. They will begin downloading to your computer.

Meet the Author

Heather Wolpert-Gawron is an award-winning middle school teacher who also writes a popular education blog as Tweenteacher. She has authored a number of series of workbooks: Internet Literacy for grades 3–8, Project Based Writing for grades 3–8, and Nonfiction Reading Strategies for the Common Core for grades 1–7. She is also the author of *Writing Behind Every Door: Teaching Common Core Writing Across the Content Areas* and *'Tween Crayons and Curfews: Tips for Middle School Teachers*, both written for Routledge/Eye On Education Publishing.

Heather is a staff blogger for The George Lucas Educational Foundation's Edutopia.org. She is a Fellow of the National Writing Project, and is devoted to helping teachers regain control of their profession through elevating their practice and educating themselves on policy. She is passionate about educational technology and blended learning, and she works to help tech tentative teachers become more savvy online and off.

Heather is dedicated to a new educative movement, one that casts teachers in the roles of curriculum designers and archivists. She believes teachers have a vital role to play in K12 instructional design.

She is wife to Royce, whom she met in 2nd grade, after karate-chopping him at recess. Additionally, she is mom to eight-year-old Benjamin and three-year-old Samwise (yes, like the Hobbit) whom they call Sam. She lives with all her boys and their boxer/corgi mix, their laughter and chaos, in Los Angeles, CA.

Foreword

Suzie Boss

So, a guy walks into an elevator and asks, "What the heck *is* Project Based Learning anyway?"

Unbelievable? Not if the storyteller is Heather Wolpert-Gawron. This inspiring educator is on a mission to make learning meaningful, motivating, and enjoyable for students and teachers alike. Project Based Learning (PBL) is her method. In the classroom, she leverages everything in her toolkit, from anecdotes to authentic assessment strategies, to cause her students "to feel something, sensing in themselves their own growth."

With her *DIY Project Based Learning* books, Heather opens up that extensive toolkit and invites fellow teachers to take a look—and borrow liberally. It's a generous move by a teacher who has worked hard to develop her own, deep understanding of PBL and to design projects that resonate with students.

From working with teachers interested in PBL myself, I know that newcomers to this instructional approach benefit from examples. Few of us, after all, had a chance to learn this way when we were students. Some teachers struggle to imagine how they can guide students through engaging project experiences and also meet serious learning goals.

Heather paints a vivid picture. As she describes her creative process for designing academically rigorous projects, I can imagine sharing a table with her at her favorite tea shop and talking through project ideas together.

The projects Heather brings into her middle-school classroom align with Common Core State Standards. But that's not where her design process begins. As she explains, "Frankly, I'm selfish. I prefer to enjoy what I'm doing. I want to be excited about what I'm about to present to the kids. That way, my excitement trickles down to my students. Working with the standards at the forefront of my mind and the content in the background is a stinky model. I prefer to flip that way of thinking." She recommends designing "towards what you love. Think about your own interests and the interests of your students." From there, it's a matter of looking at the standards and finding a good fit.

Heather deconstructs several of her classroom-tested projects to show how PBL unfolds, from start to finish. She gets into the nitty-gritty, with specific details about the teaching strategies and learning activities she incorporates into each project to build students' mastery of concepts. She shares the tools that help her students manage their time, along with the digital tools that she integrates to take learning deeper. Want to learn how to leverage a Twitter backchannel or do a collaborative writing activity using Google Docs? She shows how it's done. For anyone curious about the outcomes of PBL, Heather also offers samples of student work.

There's more advice here on everything from how to assign homework to how to plan authentic assessment. The second half of the book is packed with templates and tools just waiting for you to borrow and incorporate in your next project.

Along with the excellent advice she packs into these pages, Heather infuses her writing with personality, humor, and reflection. She shows by example why teachers shouldn't hesitate to bring their passion and humor into the classroom. She also makes a convincing case for collaborating with colleagues to expand PBL possibilities.

Many teachers find their way to PBL out of a desire to give students more voice and choice in their education. What does that mean in practice? For starters, Heather recommends being transparent with students about the big picture of any project. Let students know what's coming up, including the assessment plan. She also reminds us of the value of peer-to-peer learning. As she explains, "Students must be taught how to teach. They must learn to teach each other, and in so doing, will learn to teach themselves. After all, education's job is not to always be there for the student, but to give them the skills to be their own source of education during their life."

What do students have to say about this approach to learning? Here's one of my favorite comments, from a student named Daniel: "What I think engages a student most is interactions with real-life dilemmas and an opportunity to learn how to solve them . . . Something so interesting that you could never, ever forget."

PBL is still the exception in most classrooms. With Heather's inspiration and guidance, more students can look forward to taking part in unforgettable learning adventures.

Suzie Boss
Education Consultant and National Faculty Member
for the Buck Institute for Education Portland, Oregon

Introduction

When you first get into the swing of teaching, I mean, when you first really start feeling like you know what you're doing, your next step is to figure out what you really love about teaching. I'm not talking about why you do it. We all teach for many reasons: we love the students, we want to give back, we want to pass on a passion for a subject that we love, we want a reliable paycheck. All are great reasons to love teaching.

But it takes a while to get good enough at the science of teaching to then decide what you really love about it. For me, it's curriculum design. I love telling a story through the lessons I design. I love developing units that really connect with kids, that really help them learn to communicate, and that really leverage the love of learning in order to achieve. Many Saturdays, one can find me at The Chado Tearoom in Pasadena, CA, laptop opened, clicking away, for hours at a time, devising some new unit of study for my students. The waitresses who know me are kind enough to seat me away from the main restaurant area and keep the tea and finger sandwiches coming until I rise from my dreamlike state of curriculum design. For me, imagining curriculum is like writing a tale of learning, and I can get lost in it.

I'm like a student myself. Sometimes I write something that makes me laugh out loud, or sometimes I come a across a resource that makes me cry, one that I can see in the hands of my middle schoolers, causing them to feel something, sensing in themselves their own growth, and hopefully instilling in them a desire to share and communicate that resource with others much like I want to share it with them.

When I was a new teacher, I found that many resources that were adopted in the classroom bored me to a different set of tears. I grew frustrated. I'd think: *how can I transfer a love of learning of what I'm teaching if I don't emotionally connect with the material?*

I didn't understand why so many history textbooks were third person, dry retellings of what could be amazing tales of true-life heroism and progress. I didn't understand why, as much as I liked literature, Language Arts wasn't more about the Art of Using Language.

Why couldn't we learn to communicate multiple content areas of our choice? Why did we always have to analyze books of our school's choosing or short stories from some pacing guide if those narratives didn't resonate with students or with me, the teacher?

And as a teacher, it slowly made me mad.

Life is storytelling, and I always wondered why our lessons and units couldn't tell stories as well. Why couldn't a unit be a vehicle for lessons that have a sense of purpose? Why couldn't an assessment be more about the journey of learning than the snapshot-one-day-test to see what was learned? After all, much like becoming physically healthy, learning should be a slower process if it's going to be long lasting. A quick series of lessons followed by a test is, as is going on a crash diet and then quickly defaulting back to weight gain, sure to result in equally temporary learning.

So soon after I became a teacher, I found myself in my first teashop, surrounded by the required textbooks, and designing units that told stories. Stories about life, stories about achievement, stories about problem and solution.

I had stumbled on a passion for developing units submerged in Project Based Learning.

I found that there were others like me, other teachers who loved to tackle a wider and deeper methodology of teaching and learning. But few were actually designing these units themselves. I began field testing my units with other teachers, finding those that worked only for my students because of my own understanding of how to build the units, and finding those that seemed to work in many classrooms, not just those in which I delivered the instructions.

This book represents some of my most popular units and the lessons that can be worked into any number of them. After all, one can pick up a book on Project Based Learning, but many of them out there are about the rationale of PBL, not the day-to-day implementation of it. This book, on the other hand, gives you both. And with access to the Why and the How, I hope that my passion for curriculum design is one that will help transform your own classroom.

Project Based Learning, the Common Core, and the 4Cs

You know the hardest thing about teaching using PBL? Explaining it to someone. It seems to me that whenever I asked someone the definition of PBL, it was always so complicated a description that my eyes would begin to glaze over immediately. So to help you in your own musings, I've devised an elevator speech to help you clearly see what's it all about.

An elevator speech is a brief one- or two-sentence answer that you could give someone in the amount of time it takes to go from the first floor to the second floor in an apartment building. I like this visual, and I use it with my students, because getting to the point and encapsulating the gist of something is vital in today's speaking and writing-heavy world.

OK, so the elevator opens up, a guy walks in, and out of the blue asks you, "What the heck *is* Project Based Learning anyway?" I don't know why he would ask that, but for the purposes of this fantasy it seems that any Joe off the street is fascinated by your response.

You respond accordingly. "PBL is the act of learning through identifying a real world problem and developing its solution. Kids show what they learn as they journey through the unit, not just at the end."

"That's it?" the guy asks.

"Well, no," you reply. "There's more to it than that, but this is your floor and we're out of time." He gives you a brief nod of thanks and departs, leaving you to think of all the richness that this definition does not, in fact, impart.

After all, if we just look at that definition, it doesn't state certain trends in PBL. So now that it's just you (the reader) and I talking, let's bump up that definition so that it more accurately captures the power of this learning strategy.

PBL is the *ongoing* act of learning *about different subjects simultaneously. This is achieved by guiding students to identify, through research,* a real world problem, *local to global,* developing its solution *using evidence to support the claim, and offering the solution using a multimedia approach to presentation using skills based in a 21st-century set of tools.* Kids show what they learn as they journey through the unit, *interact with its lessons, collaborate with each other, and assess themselves and each other. They don't just take a test or produce a product* at the end *to show their learning.*

You realize that this definition, while closer to accurate than the previous version, would have caused his eyes to glaze over, and you decide that the earlier definition is by far the more efficient version, even as it shortchanges the awesomeness of the strategy.

It is exciting to teach using PBL, and that excitement of yours, in turn, causes excitement in your clients, the students.

Nevertheless, it took me a while to tease myself away from the daily drudge of teaching with disconnected lessons. You know what I mean. I'm talking about the daily lessons that might teach a skill, and perhaps that skill fits within a unit based on a topic or a theme, but each lesson works independently and can function without being embraced in a unit that connects them all in a learning story.

But I grew bored, and I was concerned that my students would too.

Teaching using PBL is the difference between the atmosphere at Disneyland and the atmosphere at a Six Flags resort. No offense to Six Flags, but their décor needs some serious work. At Disneyland, you are submerged in the story of each ride from the time you enter the line. The walls, the ceiling, the ground on which you trod as you advance to the actual ride, all supports the end result.

Teaching with PBL is much the same way. It couches lessons in a tale, a tale about a problem that must be solved or an activity that must be developed. The learning happens along the way towards the presentation of the solution. Along the way, students are asked to do any of the following:

1. question
2. research
3. write
4. speak
5. solve
6. work together
7. argue
8. analyze
9. advocate
10. synthesize.

This list goes on and on. But when you think about the Common Core standards and the 4Cs, it's clear that PBL hits them all, almost without thinking about it.

According to the Partnership for 21st Century Learning, the skills of tomorrow are as follows:

- ◆ questioning
- ◆ independent learning
- ◆ compromise
- ◆ summarizing
- ◆ sharing the air
- ◆ persuading
- ◆ goal setting
- ◆ collaboration
- ◆ communication

- ◆ problem solving
- ◆ decision making
- ◆ understanding bias
- ◆ leadership.

You can also categorize future skills by simply dividing them up into the 4Cs: Collaboration, Communication, Critical Thinking, and Creativity; all of which are hit with any PBL unit.

Testing needs to move beyond the simple multiple choice and into a more performance-based assessment as we are seeing in the Common Core tests around the country. PBL is, in a sense, an extended performance based assessment; one that is deeper and richer and, as a by-product, makes students more flexible and more aware of the alternative methods of communicating knowledge.

After all, using Project Based Learning isn't about writing a state report. It's about using what you know about the state you study and then creating your own state.

It isn't about building a replica of the Washington monument. It's about researching someone to honor, designing your own monument, and persuasively pitching a committee to build it.

Project Based Learning typically is grounded in the following elements:

- ◆ role-playing
- ◆ real world scenarios
- ◆ blended writing genres
- ◆ multiple reading genres
- ◆ authentic assessments
- ◆ authentic audiences
- ◆ real world expertise brought into the classroom
- ◆ units that assess multiple skills
- ◆ units require research and comprehension of multiple subjects.

Allow me to personify for a moment: PBL cares about our mission to educate all. PBL never forgets that one of our main jobs is to prepare students for the predicted future. PBL knows that students are not standardized, they don't learn in a standardized way, and that our clientele can't be assessed in a standardized manner if we are looking to foster innovation. PBL keeps its eye on the ball no matter the trendy standard or curriculum package du jour.

Experts Weigh In

In my own journey towards total Project Based Learning implementation, I met many along the way who feel as I do. In fact, it seems you can't click open your SmartBrief without seeing some article or post that highlights different aspects of Project Based Learning.

Different people have different reasons for using PBL, but they all recognize its importance in developing problem solving and addressing the need to bring more of the real world into the classroom.

In A.J. Juliani's book, *Inquiry and Innovation* (Routledge, 2014), he focuses on modeling methods in the classroom that work in the business world as well (like Google's 20% creative time theory of productivity). He also goes into detail about predicting what the world might be like years from now when our students graduate into its clutches. He predicts that we will soon have

> a workplace that is more individualized and personalized than ever before . . . We've seen the shift, as Fortune 500 companies have begun embracing strategies used in start-ups. Those startups like Google, Apple, and Microsoft were all founded by innovators who believe in the power of inquiry . . . Without inquiry there is little to no innovation. It's our job in education to free up time for innovation. It's our job to open their minds to new ideas. It's our job to prepare them for the present and future possibilities.

Juliani also questions the traditional model of education when he predicts that many future jobs will be more heuristic in nature. He explains that

> an algorithmic task is one in which you follow a set of established instructions down a single pathway to one conclusion. A heuristic task involves trial and error and discovering the solution by yourself. . . . Heuristic jobs involve creativity and doing something new often.

Sounds like PBL to me.

Project Based Learning is also catching on in other organizations as well. Mike Kyle is a former CEO who left the entertainment and marketing industry to launch an after-school facility dedicated to his childhood passion for forensics. His Speech and Debate academy, Nova42, incorporates Project Based Learning in much of what they do. Unlike many after school academies, Nova42 isn't just drill-and-kill, rows and rows of students working towards competition at the expense of the learning, as many private debate organizations can be. Kyle says:

> When I am able to apply the lesson or exercise to a real world event (such as a job or college interview) the student becomes much more engaged and shows more focus than if I were to simply lecture the importance. We often use role playing and real world adult mentors to make it even more powerful.

Then there are those who see the benefit of using PBL when studying through the lens of teacher quality as well. When asked about why teachers should play an integral part in creating these PBL units, Barnett Barry, a key author of *Teacherpreneurs* (Jossey-Bass, 2013) and CEO of the Center for Teaching Quality, explains that "research shows that when teachers are involved in project-based learning, their students score higher on complex measures of academic achievement. We also know that when teachers are more engaged in designing their own work students are more excited about schooling."

In fact, David Orphal, a gifted teacher and member of the Center of Teachi about PBL in his 2014 EdWeek article, explaining that "nearly all of our wor so I try as often as possible to give students an authentic audience for their students far more enthusiastic and invested in the outcome of their project."

Tony Wagner, expert in residence at Harvard's Innovation Lab, reported in a blog for MindShift in 2014 that "Content knowledge has to be engaging to kids. If kids aren't motivated, you can pour content knowledge in their heads and it comes right out the other ear . . . Above all, they need to be creative problem solvers." He continues, "Students are learning many more real world skills, as well as content knowledge, through projects . . . They're doing work worth doing. They're doing work that's interesting, and engaging."

The most important experts of them all, of course, are the clients themselves. What do students think about learning through a Project Based Learning unit?

To answer that question, after teaching a PBL unit based on the TED conference model (see my book *DIY Project Based Learning for Math and Science*), I asked students to reflect on what worked and what didn't. Surveying the students makes them more aware of the process in which they learned. After all, when one is learning in an engaged way, sometimes the cogs in the machine are invisible to the driver. I wanted to make sure that the unit was more transparent, so at the end, I reviewed the list of lessons and skills that we covered to make it all happen. This not only serves to embed the content more deeply, but what results from the review is an unveiling of sorts of the bones of the story we have told together.

So I asked students to share their thoughts on whether they felt they learned more using these methods. What they describe, I believe, is more convincing than the statements from a room full of academic experts, as to why it is vital to use PBL in the classroom.

Sofia: *"I believe that it all boils down to relationships. Not relationships from teacher to student or relationships from student to student, but rather relations between the text and the outside world. [PBL] . . . brought me to a greater thinking, a kind of thinking where I can relate the past to the present and how closely they are bonded together."*

Yvette: *"If you relate the topic to the students' lives, then it makes the concept easier to grasp."*

Jason: *"Students are most interested when the curriculum applies to more than just the textbook. The book is there—we can read a book. If we're given projects that expand into other subjects and make us think, it'll help us understand the information."*

Daniel: *"What I think engages a student most is interactions with real-life dilemmas and an opportunity to learn how to solve them. Also, projects that are unique and one-of-a-kind that other schools would never think of. Also something challenging and not easy, something to test your strengths as a student and stimulate your brain, so it becomes easier to deal with similar problems when you are grown up and have a job. Something so interesting that you could never, ever forget."*

Natalie: *"I like to explore beyond the range of what normal textbooks allow us to do through hands-on techniques such as project-based learning. Whenever I do a project, I always seem to remember the material better than if I just read the information straight out of a textbook."*

Kevin: *"I, myself, find a deeper connection when I'm able to see what I'm learning about eye-to-eye. It's more memorable and interesting to see all the contours and details of it all. To be able to understand and connect with the moment is what will make students three times more enthusiastic about learning beyond the black and white of the Times New Roman text."*

The Relationship between PBL and Teaching Writing

One of the most exciting elements about teaching with Project Based Learning is that so many subjects can be potentially woven into any given unit. This makes it more fascinating for you and for the students because you are all learning together. They are learning how to communicate the content, and you are learning more about other subject areas than you would have learned had you just stuck to your old textbook. It's stimulating.

But the one common subject that weaves through any unit, in any classroom, is writing. In fact, we can almost call PBL Project Based Writing simply because no matter the lens through which you are learning, be it from a scientific standpoint, a mathematical methodology, or a literary lens, writing is still necessary. As I say in my workbook, "Project Based Writing" (Teacher Created Resources, 2010),

> any subject, be it Language Arts or STEM, can benefit from strong writing practice. Any genre of writing can support the other ... The multi-genre aspect of Project-based writing is an important one because it is vital that students understand that genres are not compartmentalized in life. A narrative can support a persuasive argument; just as digital photography or graphs can support a summary or response to Literature. Weaving these genres together into a multi-genre project is the key to Project-based writing.

No matter the subject, writing is the main vehicle that houses the communication of that content. After all, no scientist proposing the existence of a new particle can avoid writing about it. No historian looking to debate the cause of a war or a mathematician looking to suggest a solution can avoid writing about it. PBL supports the use of additional writing skills regardless of whether the end result of a unit asks students to record themselves (they still need to write a script) or present a speech (they still need to write an advocacy essay).

For instance, I stumbled on a little PBL unit years ago when an opportunity came up to improve the overall school environment by changing the bell tone. If we failed, I figured, we would have still learned something. If we succeeded, we'd be the heroes on a campus that was plagued with an annoying bell.

As I wrote in my book, *'Tween Crayons and Curfews: Tips for Middle School Teachers*, "PBL has the student develop an authentic goal that requires authentic skills in which to achieve it." Considering our new school bell was terrible, we, as a class, decided that we might be able to change it. As I wrote in the book, the bell sounded like

> this synthesized Big Ben wanna-be chime that we hear no less than 20 times a day. Furthermore, it's unsynchronized. That is, it functions like a rolling earthquake (a little shout-out to all those California teachers out there) in that it rings first in one wing of the school and then makes its way down campus in an echo-like roll of Casio-esque horror.

> My students decided to take matters into their own hands and use Persuasive writing to beg the powers that be to change our bell. Now, it just so happens that the new computer routers for the school are located in the back of my room and the new bell is housed in the mounted big black box. Therefore, when the maintenance crew came in one day for something, I simply asked, "Hey, is there a choice of bells up there?" They foolishly said yes, and thus began a Persuasive writing unit of Project-Based Learning.

We researched the kind of computer routers that were housed in the back of the room to eliminate any possible "no" based on technical ignorance on our part.

We worked on persuasive letter writing, knowing that we would have to petition the administration for the change of bell. These letters not only worked on business letter formatting, but also made sure to include a thesis, a counterargument, and a call to action.

We graphed results of polls of students and teachers to use as evidence, and readied a panel of students who would present the proposal. We also worked on different kinds of visual presentations, finally voting on the best one, that would back up the oral presentation to admin.

Even while our spontaneous project embraced math and technology and oral presentation, writing was the main method used to communicate our content.

How to Create Your Own PBL Unit Focusing on ELA and/or History

Call me bass-ackwards, but I don't design projects around the Common Core Standards; I design projects based on what I believe are engaging topics that encourage my curriculum. Having said that, I don't neglect them either. In fact, by the end of my design process, I would say that I've become rather intimate with the series of standards I'm trying to hit.

Project Based Learning is very different from just assigning projects. Assigning a project is a simple assessment. PBL, however, is the unit that encompasses all of the lessons, all of the explorations, the research, and the delivery of a solution that the students are trying to present. Driven by an essential or guided question, a PBL unit may culminate in a "project" in order to be the vehicle of the information being presented, but the end result isn't the proof of the learning. What is accomplished on the journey, however, is. It's about the process, not the end project.

In fact, designing and developing a Project Based Learning outcome is its own process, and while I don't tend to invite the standards to the party first off, they do end up being the guest of honor.

Now, I have a two-prong approach to designing PBL units or even developing the Performance Based Assessments for my own district. The first way, of course, is to look at the standards and work through each trying to sometimes fit a square peg in a round hole.

I prefer, however, a different way to design. I think about what I would enjoy first and then backplan from there.

Remember, some of what PBL can offer is enthusiasm for learning and, frankly, I'm selfish. I prefer to enjoy what I'm doing. I want to be excited about what I'm about to present to the kids. That way, my excitement trickles down to my students. Working with the standards at the forefront of my mind and the content in the background is a stinky model. I prefer to flip that way of thinking.

For instance, when I first began building my Superhero Project Based Learning unit (see Chapter 1), a unit based on developing origin stories and advocacy speeches to a mythical United Nations, I didn't think at all about the Common Core Standards until my checklists and lessons were designed and in front of my face.

I knew I wanted my students to write origin stories as their narratives. I knew I wanted them to watch TED speeches and model their blended-genre, advocacy presentations on those that included elements of memoir, persuasion, incorporated digital media, and website design.

But once the unit had been created, I knew that the next step was to see what standards my enthusiasm had hit all by itself. I developed a little checklist of Common Core Standards that I keep tacked up on my corkboard for just such moments.

Using that tool, I saw that all on my own, I had hit key standards for my ELA class. For instance, just based on the basic genres my unit was covering, I knew that I had hit:

CCSS.ELA-LITERACY.W.8.1
Write arguments to support claims with clear reasons and relevant evidence.

CCSS.ELA-LITERACY.W.8.2
Write informative/explanatory texts to examine a topic and convey ideas, concepts, and information through the selection, organization, and analysis of relevant content.

CCSS.ELA-LITERACY.W.8.3
Write narratives to develop real or imagined experiences or events using effective technique, relevant descriptive details, and well-structured event sequences.

I also knew that I would walk the students through the writing process multiple times throughout the unit. So I knew that I had hit:

CCSS.ELA-LITERACY.W.8.5
With some guidance and support from peers and adults, develop and strengthen writing as needed by planning, revising, editing, rewriting, or trying a new approach, focusing on how well purpose and audience have been addressed.

But once done, I looked at the matrix of standards and I looked at my lessons and student objectives, and I realized that I hadn't naturally gravitated towards something like

CCSS.ELA-LITERACY.W.8.2.A
Introduce a topic clearly, previewing what is to follow; organize ideas, concepts, and information into broader categories; include formatting (e.g., headings), graphics (e.g., charts, tables), and multimedia when useful to aiding comprehension.

So I backplanned and put in a lesson that asked students to develop infographics about their advocacy topic. They needed to embed subheadings into their argument, dividing up their topics. To support each subheading, they were required to provide evidence, not only in textual references, but also in visual graphics. They created a visual using Piktochart.com, incorporating text, icons, and data to support their problems and proposed solutions.

To summarize, it becomes a basic process made up of three steps:

1. Design towards what you love. Think about your own interests and the interests of the age group you teach.
2. Look back at the Common Core Standards.
3. Fill in the gaps.

Of course, it's not always possible to fill in every gap. After all, at least in secondary, you really are limited by time. So that's where cross-curricular planning comes in. Find someone to partner with who might share your interest in your unit; or, look towards what other subjects are doing at your grade level and see if their curriculum naturally fills the gaps in your own matrix.

After all, we have to remember that we aren't the only ones with our hands on those students during their school year. There are others who, combining forces with your efforts, can share the burden of hitting those standards.

It's vital we collaborate. It's vital that we open our doors and utilize the strengths of a team of teachers per student. The Standards are broad and vast and deep, so much so that one teacher cannot possibly hit them all with the depth necessary for true learning and transfer.

That being said, I begin developing a unit by creating a checklist.

Developing and providing checklists speaks to college and career readiness in the Common Core. After all, organization, preparedness, goal setting, and the independent learning that comes from utilizing resources are all folded into the expectations of these new standards.

But they also hit 21st-century skills and strategies presented by such websites as The Institute of Museum and Library Services that calls for the following:

Manage Projects (Productivity and Accountability)
◆ Set and meet goals, even in the face of obstacles and competing pressures.
◆ Prioritize, plan, and manage work to achieve the intended result.

Manage Goals and Time (Initiative And Self-Direction)
◆ Set goals with tangible and intangible success criteria.
◆ Balance tactical (short-term) and strategic (long-term) goals.
◆ Utilize time and manage workload efficiently.

It's about transparency, and the more information you grant to students, the better. After all, if we're working to let go of the authority in the room and create a classroom where students own their learning, then we have to let them in on the sequence of lessons and assessments ahead of time. There's no reason why students should be in the dark as to what I will expect and why. The mystery defeats achievement.

There are many reasons to use checklists:

1. they make sense of the big picture of a particular unit
2. they help me plan ahead, forcing me to think about where I want to go and how
3. they communicate to parents what we are doing in the classroom so that there aren't mixed messages coming home regarding the purpose or pacing of assignments
4. they provide students a resource to develop better time management skills by planning and prepping assignments in advance.

Some checklists I provide are fully filled out in advance and copied (or shared via Google Drive). Others allow for students to fill them in. We sit down at the top of a unit and spend a period going through what will be required. I find that students have more ownership when it's in their own writing or typing, so it's time well spent. I have even, on occasion, permitted students to set their own deadlines on their checklists. However, once it's filled in, it acts like a contract, and that student must meet that deadline specified.

When developing your own checklists, make sure you backplan. When do you want the final assessment/presentation to be? Enter that date first on your checklist. Then fill it in from there, making predications about how long it might take for you and students to accomplish particular tasks.

I always include a cover sheet that informs all stakeholders (students, parents and administration) of the intention of a particular unit. This also includes a contact email or phone number where I can be reached with questions.

The table itself should also have a few empty rows. This goes hand in hand with a front-loaded conversation you need to have with students about being flexible. I consider flexibility another 21st-century skill. After all, you can only predict so well. You must tell students that while these assignments reflect the overall goals and lessons planned at this time, you still have the right as their guide to cross an assignment off the list or add one if you discover a gap in the learning once the unit begins. It's your call, and it's an all-important lesson in being flexible.

It's like a contract. You promise to think ahead, not to wing it, and be transparent with your plans. They, on the other hand, promise to plan ahead. So, as a teacher, you don't need to get too compulsive about providing every beat of a unit ahead of time. Your goal is to grant them access to your thought process that exists to the best of your knowledge at this time.

So, what do students think of checklists? Well, I asked them, and they said the following:

Joshua: *Our checklists give us a visual list of what we have to do. For example, a checklist would be better than paragraph instructions because we have to draw out a list from a paragraph, whereas in a checklist, we can immediately see what we need to do and get straight to work.*

Destiny: *I am a procrastinator, and having the kind of motivation to check something off is great for me to stay on track . . . It's like if you have 10 parts of your assignment, for every one you check off, it's like a small victory.*

Alyssa: *Checklists let me know about big assessments that may come in the future and allow me to plan for them. Checklists also keep me organized and help me remember what I have due and when for long-term projects.*

Caitlin: *The human mind can become forgetful, and checklists help keep track of many things and ease the pressure of remembering certain things . . . They help you avoid minor/major mistakes.*

I mention checklists because they are vital to the organization and structure of a PBL unit. For, as any teacher who uses PBL can tell you, it can get unstructured pretty darn fast if you don't have some kind of scaffolding holding the organization of the unit intact.

To fill in that checklist with lessons, informal, and formal assessments, takes pulling from a toolbox of activities. Think of this book as a kind of toolbox from which you can draw.

How This Book Is Different from Other PBL Books

Many PBL books are about using it Someday, not Monday. This book is meant to give you rationale and enthusiasm, to be sure, but it's also meant to get you started right away.

As I have said in my previous book, *Writing Behind Every Door: Teaching Common Core Writing in the Content Areas*, "If it doesn't exist outside of school, then it isn't worthy enough to be taught within school." Project-Based Learning focuses on this mantra, and this book will provide methods that teachers can use to follow through with its promise.

You'll find that this book is made up of two parts. These two parts can be combined to form any number of different PBL units.

The first part of this book is full of complete units. They include:

1. overviews and descriptions of a whole unit, the goals and objectives
2. FAQs about the unit: subjects that are integrated, skills used, etc.
3. step-by-step and day-to-day guides towards implementing the unit including simple scripts if necessary and handouts as needed
4. student samples
5. targeted rubrics as necessary.

I've also included something called "Homework Hints." Sometimes with PBL, teachers get a little lost in the most traditional of assignments, homework. Throughout this book, I've indicated opportunities to assign independent take home assignments that can be used to fulfill this requirement if you need it.

Each unit also contains a checklist or pacing guide of assignments to act as a skeleton to guide both you and your students through a particular unit.

The second part of this book includes a whole stack of resources that can be inserted into existing units or combined to create new and exciting ones or your own creation.

If you know that your students need to brush up on something such as Researching Online Reliably, for instance, I've got a lesson for that. If you find you need your students to use a typical outline for writing an argument, something that ELA teaches, but other subject area teachers typically don't, there's one in here as well.

This structure allows you to mix and match your lessons to meet the needs of your students. It also allows you to tweak what I've developed and make a PBL concoction all your own.

Incidentally, many of these lessons are stand-alone activities or resources, so feel free to use them outside of the realm of PBL. However, I would recommend housing them within a PBL unit so that they have a full impact on the learner.

I hope that this book helps you learn through doing. Don't wait to invent a unit yourself; look to mine as a way in to PBL. Then, I challenge you to go out and tweak, revise, and create yourself. You won't regret it as a teacher, and you won't regret it as a learner either.

Part I

PBL Units

The Superhero Unit

A unit based on superhero science, science-fiction narratives, and advocacy writing, culminating in an issues-based presentation to the "United Nations."

Table 1.1 Superhero Unit Facts

Subjects Integrated	Writing: narrative, advocacy, executive summary
	Science: student choice
	Reading: informational
	Technology: website design, Twitter, word processing, Internet literacy for research, presentations, infographics, online ethics, hyperlinking
	Art: student choice
	Oral presentation
Skills Used	Collaboration
	Problem solving
	Creativity
	Communication
	Critical thinking
	Questioning
Duration	One quarter–one semester
Driving Question	What makes a hero?

Overview

This totally immersive unit can span up to a full semester or be accomplished in less time, depending on the lessons utilized.

The Superhero Unit is an extensive PBL unit that focuses on student role-play. The first quarter focuses on fact-based narrative writing and internet research. Students will develop a new superhero character and write a science fiction-based origin story about that persona. They will also develop an informational newspaper article that reports on the How, What, Where, When, and Why of an event signaling the first sighting of that superhero in action.

The second quarter focuses on advocacy writing and oral speaking. The superhero characters developed earlier in the semester are then tasked to find an issue that relates to his or her superpowers or origin story. (For instance, because of Aquaman's relationship to water, he might support the fight against ocean pollution.) The student must research that problem (local, state, national, or international) and research or devise a possible solution. They then must pitch their solution (in costume, of course) to an audience made up of ambassadors to the United Nations.

Meanwhile, the students in the audience will be roleplaying as the ambassadors themselves. Prior to the presentation, the students will all have previously researched different countries, so that they might, as a UN body, then vote on which superhero's problem/solution they should fund. Therefore, both the student presenter is role-playing during their pitch to the UN, while the audience members are also role-playing as ambassadors from a country randomly assigned to them.

The elements of PBL this unit supports are as follows:

◆ blended writing genres
◆ experts in the classroom
◆ oral presentation
◆ role-play
◆ subject integration
◆ advocacy/problem-solution
◆ collaboration
◆ real world connections.

It is a long-lasting and deep-thinking unit that submerges the students in engaging role-play, fueled by the buy-in of student choice, and propelled through the academic rigor of research and communication skills.

Step-by-Step Lessons

As with many PBL units, you want to start each with a bang. I start this narrative-focused unit with a short iMovie, set to music, which introduces the students immediately to the character and heart of the unit. This sets the tone of the overarching project.

The short presentation will show images of superheroes, photographs and animated images, set to an excerpt from John Williams' Superman main title sequence. It's a great score. The text in the iMovie will say the following:

This school year, you are embarking on an adventure. Are you up for the challenge of a lifetime?

If you were a superhero, who would you be?
If you were a superhero, what would you stand for?
If you were a superhero, what would be your superpower?
If you were a superhero, what would be your Achilles heel, your weakness?
If you were a superhero, for whom would you fight?

Welcome to 8th grade, and the Semester of the Superheroes . . .

In time for the second quarter and advocacy, I then join them in the role-play, producing another short video, this time with me as the chairman of the United Nations calling on their superhero to help fix the problems of the planet. I like roleplaying too, after all. Why should the students get to have all the fun?

Back to first quarter. Once the motivational iMovie has been viewed, it's time to get down to business. I pass out a checklist of assignments that give the students an overview of what will be expected of them this quarter. The checklist is intended to both help students with time management and communicate to parents and families about the rationale of the unit. This will give the students an overview of the work they will need to accomplish and the deadline for different tasks. I'll be giving them time in class to work through it all, with homework being reserved for assignments not finished in the 45 minutes we have together daily. I'm not a big homework fan otherwise.

ELA First Quarter Checklist: Narrative

All superheroes came from somewhere. Where they came from and how they became heroes are called origin stories. A great origin story isn't just about writing a fun story. Believable origin stories are seeded with facts. In this case, you will be given the choice of writing a science fiction story or a historical fiction story. This will take research as well as a thorough knowledge of your character and his or her abilities, foibles, and background.

Table 1.2 First Quarter Checklist

Assigned	Assignment	Due	How to Submit
	Inquiry chart Science fiction (Classwork)	N/A	
	Select book (bring it in daily)		
	Finish book		
	Character analysis		
	Research check #1 Bibliography uses MLA or APA format http://owl.english.purdue.edu/owl/resource/560/01/ http://www.easybib.com/		
	Research check #2 Bibliography uses MLA or APA format		
	Pixar's rules of storytelling analysis http://i.imgur.com/DH1lF.jpg		
	16 fancy literary techniques explained by Disney		
	Google advanced search screen shot due		
	Linking text		
	TED speeches notes check		
	Hooks and The Bulwer-Lytton Fiction Contest (http://www.bulwer-lytton.com/)		
	Grammar lessons (https://www.youtube.com/watch?v=Ry-NYbMEbgc&sns=fb) – Google Matrix Assignment		
	Rough draft narrative due		
	Final draft narrative due		
	Finding different text structures in a real-world text		
	Newspaper article due		

(continued on the next page)

Throughout the course of this first quarter, we will be working towards the goal of refining our skills as narrative and informational writers. To do so, we are using this checklist as a means to remain organized and on task. This checklist should be at school every day, as sometimes things will be deleted, dates might adjust, or assignments may be added. I ask that you be flexible. Note: being flexible is far easier if you don't leave assignments to the last minute.

This unit honors the 4Cs: Creativity, Collaboration, Critical Thinking, and Communication. It also expects that you submit some assignments online and some in class. You have access to me daily, so make sure that you have questions answered and issues resolved, so you can hit deadlines on time.

I have included links as resources to help in your own independent learning. The expectation is that you are learning with others and on your own. You are also expected to be your own advocate. Have questions? Freaking out? Talk to me. I'm your guide, and I'm here to help you achieve these goals to the best of your ability. I'm also here to push you to challenge what you think of as your best.

Good luck, and reach out to me anytime.

Mrs. Wolpert-Gawron

This letter and the checklist in Table 1.2 give students and families an overview, but the real teaching starts when you dive in and get your hands dirty with the lessons and deadlines.

1 **Pick a book**: within five days, a student needs to select a science-fiction novel to read in conjunction with the unit as it unfolds. The goal is to be reading a science-fiction book while writing a science-fiction origin story. The students can be inspired by the elements in their book, and the reading reinforces the writing.

Somewhere within the unit, periodically ask to see summaries or the like proving their progress through the book. Their final assignment should be a dual-entry journal in which they identify 10 real science facts and 10 science-fiction "facts" from their book described using quotes from the text. Read the students to see how long they will need in order to accomplish this task.

2 **Brush up on narrative writing**: the superhero unit begins with students writing an origin story. An origin story is a kind of narrative that tells the tale of how the superhero came to be. In this case, it could be a story of how that person gained his or her powers, or it could be about how that character finally embraced their abilities and decided to use them for good. Now, while I spend time focusing on reviewing the elements of narrative, I also weave in time to teach high-quality informational or argumentation writing, which are both Common Core aligned and the focus of the majority of our school's writing goals. To do that, the narrative becomes the vehicle for informational facts. Hence, the focus on science-fiction and research.

But to write a good origin story, or to write even many arguments, students need a brush up on what makes a good narrative. So, while students are reading their books, the teacher can use the different independent reading books in the room to highlight the elements of good narrative writing. The teacher could do the following throughout the course of the unit:

◆ Emphasize hooks: have students bring in the first paragraph of their science-fiction book, write it on sentence strips, and post on a common board for other students to see. Another resource to use to teach about hooks is the Bulwer-Lytton Contest (see Part II, page 129). This is a contest to see who can write the most overwritten hooks imaginable. Tell students about the history of this contest, show them the funniest of examples, and have them develop their own.

◆ Review plot structure: have students plot exposition, rising action, climax, falling action, and resolution onto a document so that they can see the physical "swoop" of a story by analyzing the one they are reading.

◆ Highlight character traits: have the students create a four-square chart that breaks down the characters in his/her book. (See the graphic organizer in Part II, page 132.) It asks students to analyze a character in terms of physical description, a brief background about family, personality traits, goals and objectives, and what others might say about this character if you overheard them talking about him or her. This chart will then be used again when the students create their own characters for their superhero origin stories. Getting to know their characters is very important, as they will be working with these aliases throughout the semester; so establishing where they came from is vital to the realism and rigor of the unit as a whole.

Of course, there are other lessons you can highlight too using their independent reading books:

◆ theme
◆ figurative language
◆ word choice
◆ sentence structure and variety
◆ etc.

Two resources I use during this time of the unit are one produced by Disney and another by Pixar. After all, both of these studios are some of the best storytellers around.

The first is called 16 Fancy Literary Techniques Explained by Disney and the second is a list entitled Pixar's 22 Rules of Storytelling. The latter was created by animator Emma Coats as a list to describe Pixar's secret sauce of story telling. It's a great resource for blossoming writers.

Homework Hint

For any of these resources, you can have the students write a journal entry or blog post. Ask them: which of the following rules resonates with you? What can you see incorporating into your own writing process?

3 **Teaching research skills:** the students need to conduct a lot of research during this unit because their narrative science-fiction origin stories must be based on real science fact. There are great superhero resources out there to begin this process of research. Students can then use the resources that you provide as a jumping-off place for their own research. They can use keywords from your resources, authors from those you've provided, or just get their imagination juices going to help guide their own independent learning.

Here are a few resources to get them started:

- ◆ TED: The Science of Superheroes
- ◆ http://www.superheronation.com/2008/05/29/how-to-write-origin-stories/
- ◆ http://www.newsarama.com/15572-the-10-best-superhero-origin-stories-of-all-time.html
- ◆ http://www.readwritethink.org/resources/resource-print.html?id=30637

From there, there are tons of lessons that focus on research skills. One of the things I choose to focus on is traditional bibliographic structure. There is a lot about this unit that is not traditional; therefore, I believe that it's important to ensure that there are some lessons that are a tad uncompromising. Teaching about bibliography format is one of those. I wouldn't say it's the most engaging lesson around, but it's at this time that I teach the traditional MLA format. Well, actually, the students teach themselves. I point the way to where they can find what they need to accomplish the goal I've set of using proper format.

Depending on how you teach this, it can really support your goal towards creating independent learners. That is, if the students can figure it out themselves, why does the teacher's voice have to translate for them? Tear down the middleman and simply give students the resources. Provide them with access to the OWL website, then show them the proper way to cite major resources that they might need (a book, a website, an interview, etc.). That's when you show them something such as EasyBib, where they can enter in the information and the formatting is done for them. Why waste their time when the resource exists? From here on in, they *must* have a citation page at the end of every essay. Narrative, Argument, Executive Summary, whatever. They now must always cite. After all, with a resource like EasyBib, there's no excuse not to show your research.

During the research process is also a great time to bring in an expert speaker. Bringing experts into the classroom is also an important element with PBL. Bring in a scientist to talk to students about the physics of superheroes. Bring in a comic book writer to talk about their influences. Bring in an illustrator or another writer. The connection can be loose, but it's vital that the students hear other voices that can aid in their research. Teach students how to cite a personal interview and have them include this in their growing research library (see Homework Hint that follows).

4 **Teaching Internet literacy skills (including how to search safely):** the first mini-lesson to hit is How to Use Google Advanced Search. See Part II, page 133 for more on this lesson.

Homework Hint

Have students provide you with a screenshot of the Google Advanced Search webpage, filled in with their specific search needs. They have to take a screenshot that proves they know how to get to the Google Advanced Search page and that they know what fields to fill in more specifically to have a more efficient search. This assignment is a credit/no credit activity (partial points given for late work, of course).

Teach students about the Six Steps of Being an Internet Detective (see the handout available in Part II, page 134). Require them to practice the following:

- ◆ verify the evidence on a website by double-checking proper nouns, dates, and important keywords
- ◆ triangulate the data by finding three sites that back up a particular fact found from an initial search
- ◆ use their common sense by answering basic questions about a site (who is the author, does the author's voice sound biased, etc.)
- ◆ follow the links on a page to see if they take a reader to something such as a biased site or a for-profit one
- ◆ analyze the URL extensions to guide students about the meaning of extensions such as. com,. org,. gov.,. uk,. biz, etc. (some indicate a more reliable page than others)
- ◆ check the publisher using a medium such as easywhois.com to see if the publisher is transparent or hiding a different agenda.

Teach students also about hyperlinking. Hyperlinking is when the author creates another, more transparent level of their writing by linking keywords to their research. For instance, if a student says that her superhero has pyrokinesis (the power to move and control flames), she might link the keyword "pyrokinesis" to the HowStuffWorks website article on spontaneous human combustion, thus proving some kind of layer of research beyond her imagination.

Homework Hint

A possible homework or quiz assignment is to check the students' research by having research checks. These checks are a quick look at a growing list of bibliographical resources that students will be using to seed the facts into their origin stories. Their lists should be alphabetized and use proper MLA format. Furthermore, at the end of the unit, these bibliography lists should also correlate to the hyperlinks in the essay as well as the citations at the end of the story.

5 **Using the writing process**: according to the Common Core standards, students must write under timed circumstances as well as coaxing an essay through the writing process. That is, it must start with a rough draft, go through the revision and editing process, and appear ultimately as a final draft. Throughout the superhero unit, students will be asked to quickly write a journal entry as a means to get their writing groove going, but they also need to be writing over time.

Even the Common Core Standards distinguish the difference between short, on-the-fly writing assignments, and those given a more thorough process:

CCSS.ELA-LITERACY.W.8.5
With some guidance and support from peers and adults, develop and strengthen writing as needed by planning, revising, editing, rewriting, or trying a new approach, focusing on how well purpose and audience have been addressed.

CCSS.ELA-LITERACY.W.8.10
Write routinely over extended time frames (time for research, reflection, and revision) and shorter time frames (a single sitting or a day or two) for a range of discipline-specific tasks, purposes, and audiences.

I'm a big believer in training kids to help give feedback to each other. Frankly, with over 200 students a day, how can a teacher do it alone? That being the case, I have students collaborate throughout the writing process by exchanging essays to give feedback to one another. However, while many times it's easy for students to recognize spelling and punctuation errors (editing), it continues to be a challenge to advise students in how to give revision advice. Author and educator Kelly Gallagher came up with a great shorthand expression to help with this problem and give a tool to students looking to guidance in giving revision feedback. He writes about the RADAR strategy of revision.

RADAR stands for:

Revise: are there words that can be used that might be better than others? What can be used instead of what's been written already?
Add: what gaps exist in the story/essay that still need to be filled? Are there transitions that don't currently make sense?
Delete: what isn't needed?
and **Reorder**: should the ending be the beginning? Is this paragraph as strong as it could be in this location or should it be elsewhere? Can we shuffle the story around to make it stronger?

Another strategy kids can use when talking to each other is something such as Three Stars and a Wish. It requires students to acknowledge three pluses about a peer's essay while also requiring them to identify one area of improvement. It's simple and straightforward, and a teacher can focus the Wish requirement on a particular skill, which can give the strategy even more structure depending on the skill being taught in the classroom. So if you are a writing teacher, perhaps you can require that the wish focus on RADAR revision strategies. Then again, if you are a content area teacher, you can require that the Wish be centered on subject matter expertise.

6 **Teaching the newspaper format**: there are tons of resources out there to help teach newspaper article formatting and content. I required the following:

- ◆ a headline
- ◆ a byline
- ◆ an image with a caption
- ◆ the article itself.

To see an activity and handout that I give to the students, go to Part II, page 136.

I taught the "inverted pyramid" of newspaper writing that describes how the most important information had to be at the top of the article with information of lesser import placed towards the end. The article clearly had to focus on Who, What, Where, When, Why, and How. There needed to be a mythical witness interview as well.

Some students created one manually, but many found templates and resources online, including the template that can be found in Google Apps for Ed. It was certainly helpful to show them a template as a means to encourage more independent learning.

You can see a few examples of these newspaper articles on page 39.

7 **Creating a visual**: once they had lived and breathed their character traits for a while, it was then that I asked students to show me what their character looked like. Some drew their characters on paper, others created them digitally using a tablet and stylus, but most of them used the superhero creator on www.Marvel.com. Figures 1.1–1.4 show just a few:

Figure 1.1 Character Name: Elizabeth Hart

Eliza actually drew this one using a tablet.

Figure 1.2 Superhero Name: Gary the Bullet

Figure 1.3 Superhero Name: Volt

Both Gary the Bullet and Volt were created using the Marvel.com superhero creator.

Figure 1.4 Superhero Name: Manipulative Jessica

Of course, they can always create their superheroes by hand as well.

The second quarter smoothly transitioned into one of advocacy and oral presentation. The students were to keep their created superhero close at hand to help guide some of their decisions. The goal by the end of the quarter was to reflect back on that written origin story, incorporate what that character might feel about some of the issues that plague our world today, and select a problem that needed to be solved. Students went to great lengths to research possible solutions to that problem, provide evidence to support their own solution, and pitch that possible program to the world's ambassadors to the United Nations.

I decided that the students themselves would conduct research on different countries, the names of which were chosen from a jar, and role-play as the ambassadors themselves to become the audience for whichever character was presenting his or her problem/solution to our little "United Nations." But it took scaffolding to get them there. Hence, I developed a whole new checklist that centered on our second quarter assignments and pacing. (See Table 1.3 and the letter that introduces it.)

ELA Second Quarter Checklist: Advocacy

Continuing with our superhero-themed semester, you will be joining a league in presenting a series of issues to the United Nations. OK, so it won't be the real UN, but we will be role-playing as our superheroes (yes, I fully expect costumes the day of your presentation) and as ambassadors for a particular country.

This unit blends a lot of what we've already worked on this year: narrative, informational, and argument. Keep up with the deadlines, as we'll be moving quickly towards our final presentations.

Approach me if there are better ways you can think of to present the information than I have listed here. I want to see the best from you, so think ahead, and put in your best, most creative, most collaborative, most critical-thinking, and most communicative efforts.

Good luck, and reach out to me anytime.

Mrs. Wolpert-Gawron

Table 1.3 Second Quarter Checklist

Assigned	Assignment	Due	How to Submit
	Set up League Weebly site		
	Writing with numeracy quiz (Google Form)		
	Infographics		
	Problem statement		
	Research check #1 Bibliography uses MLA or APA format http://owl.english.purdue.edu/owl/resource/560/01/ http://www.easybib.com/		

	Research check #2 Bibliography uses MLA or APA format		
	Rough draft of advocacy speech due Writing process begins (review of RADAR)		
	Copyright and online ethics activity (Google Form)		
	About us: Weebly page (Third person group biography includes mission statement and collaboration contract)		
	Editing strategies lesson		
	Selecting a country's name		
	Research on assigned country Create a name plate with a symbol		
	Informational blog post about your assigned country		
	Research bibliography check #3		
	Final drafts due • Embedded into league website • Visuals • Infographics		
	Record your video plea and embed into website		
	Prezi or Powerpoint (three slides each); remember our guidelines! • Bullet points only, no paragraphs of text • Visually engaging based on topic and data		
	Advocacy speeches begin		
	Level 3 questions due daily by ambassadors Funding suggestion persuasive pitch due		

1 **Problem statements**: I've written about problem statements in the past. These are a summary of sorts, based on the format of those used in higher learning, that ask a student to construct a short two- or three-paragraph informational overview of a topic that they believe they may want to research further for the quarter. It also includes three to five questions about the topic that the student wants to further research. These questions help to guide future research (the questions, after all, if good enough, can seed keyword searches into Google) as the structure of their oral presentation down the line. This problem statement becomes the first step towards rigor. A student clearly has to know a certain amount about a topic in order to accomplish the assignment, and if they want their topic approved, it must be submitted with a certain level of detail. This proves, therefore, that a certain amount of research has already been done, even though the "research essay" itself hasn't even begun yet.

Although the unit I created aligns to several common core standards, it speaks really well to CCSS.ELA-Literacy.W.8.7:

Conduct short research projects to answer a question (including a self-generated question), drawing on several sources and generating additional related, focused questions that allow for multiple avenues of exploration.

The following is an example of a problem statement I use as a model. This one was origin-ally published in the workbook I wrote for Teacher Created Resources, *Project Based Writing, Grades 6–8*. You can see a student sample on page 125.

The Problem Statement

You are going to be developing what is called a "problem statement." In terms of college and career readiness, a problem statement is used anywhere from a doctorate thesis to a business proposal. It states the goal for your research and the problem you wish to solve. Ultimately, it is meant to help the focus the topic of your persuasive TED speech.

To create a problem statement, you must write a paragraph that includes the following information:

1. states the broad problem/topic about which you are interested in researching
2. defines the problem you will be solving by narrowing the issue
3. describes why it needs to be investigated by giving background information and context
4. states your goals in writing and researching this problem (I will . . ., I plan . . ., I would like . . ., I propose . . ., etc.)

From there, you will develop **three to five questions** based on the problem state-ment. These specific questions will further serve to guide your writing. By answering them through your investigation, you should then more easily find a solution or answer to your problem, which will be a main focus of your persuasive speech.

Here is an example of a completed problem statement and five corresponding questions that are specific to our speech-writing assignment. Notice how the para-graph starts out broad in its scope and narrows down to a more specific goal:

Bullying has long been a problem with children and adults alike. While bullying can be seen even in the workplace among adults, those who bully as grown-ups may also be those who bully as children. Children all over our country are victims of bullying, but bullying comes in many forms, some physical and some mental. We must combat this plague from many different angles in order to make bullies uncomfortable in their intimidation. I propose to write an Argumentation Speech that investigates the different forms of bullying and how we can band together to stop it.

Questionœs:

1. *What are the forms of bullying?*
2. *What defines bullying?*
3. *Can a bully be reformed?*
4. *What are methods a victim can use to stop being bullied?*
5. *What can schools, the government, laws, and families do to invest in solving this problem?*

Writing a problem statement at the top of many different kinds of units always fulfills the following Common Core Standard:

CCSS.ELA-LITERACY.W.8.7
Conduct short research projects to answer a question (including a self-generated question), drawing on several sources and generating additional related, focused questions that allow for multiple avenues of exploration.

2 **Writing with numeracy**: we talk a lot about students needing to embed evidence into their writing, but are we specifically teaching how to write using numbers? To counter what I felt was a gap in my own practice, I researched how mathematicians and scientists and those in higher education were solving this problem. I found a handful of rules many of them follow (and a few that were specific to particular content areas). I combined them into a reference sheet for students and tacked on a few questions for them to answer that forced them to interact and refer to the cheat sheet I'd created. You can see it in Part II on page 138.

3 **Superhero league formation**: this past year I fooled around with students creating "leagues" across the class periods. It was a huge pain, and I plan to do it differently after tweaking a few elements of the process. Nevertheless, the intention was to have students self-select their league members using some given criteria. For example, there needed to be a mix from all three class periods. Also, the superheroes couldn't repeat powers in any league; every superhero in the league had to bring something new to the party. These leagues went on to create websites together as a portfolio for the students to house all of their academic work and, in the spirit of the role-play, for their superhero counterparts to promote their advocacy issues.

Note: In the second-year incarnation of this unit, I advanced this element of the unit to permit students to solve their global problems both as individuals and as superheroes. That is, each student still needed to pitch a real-world solution complete with budget, but the characters were to also work together using their powers to inform the United Nations how they intended to solve the problem themselves. The unit in this book, however, focuses on how to guide students towards real-world solutions by each independent student.

4 **Collaboration constitution**: after the leagues were created, the groups formed by the league designs then had to create a collaboration constitution. This was a team charter of sorts, a contract that the students wrote as a group, stating their expectations for each other. They focused on the duration of time that could reasonably pass before responding to an email, the progressive steps of their own ire if someone did not carry his or her own weight, and what those consequences might be after it got to a certain point. They covered expectations on the frequency of working outside of school as well. All the league members then signed each document. The instructions for this assignment can be found in Part II, page 141.

Additionally, by the end of the unit overall, the leagues could then also develop their own collaboration rubrics to assess each other on how well they worked together. The only catch was that they could not include on the rubric an expectation that wasn't specifically spelled out in the start-of-unit constitution. Student groups designed their rubrics for free using rubistar.4teachers.org.

A student example of a Collaboration Constitution can be seen on page 37.

5 **Text structures**: we looked at the different text structures that could be found in many different writing styles and real world examples. We looked at how bold headings were used, when numbers or bullets were applicable, and when different font style decisions were appropriate and when they were distracting.

An effective video to show during this mini-lesson is based on the universality and simplicity of Helvetica. You can see it here: https://www.youtube.com/watch?v= VDLPAE9wLEU.

Here is an NPR segment on choosing the font that's right for you: http://www.npr. org/2011/09/04/140126278/know-this-headlines-font-youre-just-my-type?sc=fb&cc=fp

Homework Hint

Have students bring in an example of a print or online article that shows different text structures. This is an easy assignment to require and one that helps students see the choices in communication around them. You are asking students to recognize organizational and structural decisions that authors make everyday. Have them bring in an example of an article that uses a bulleted list or center justification. It's your choice what you want them to focus on, and they are bringing in the real-world examples.

There's a Common Core connection with this as well as seen in the following standard:

CCSS.ELA-LITERACY.W.8.2.A
Introduce a topic clearly, previewing what is to follow; organize ideas, concepts, and information into broader categories; include formatting (e.g., headings), graphics (e.g., charts, tables), and multimedia when useful to aiding comprehension.

6 **Online ethics**: teaching online ethical behavior not only hits the Common Core standards, but the "common sense" standards as well. Now, I'm not talking about manners so much as giving credit where credit is due. After all, just because the kids can access information within two clicks doesn't give them the right to claim information as their own.

So how do we as educators help students respect other people's work and not abuse it in this era of accessible information? The answer is, of course, to teach ethical academic behavior in a targeted way, to model it yourself, and to hold students accountable.

According to the Common Core Standards (CCSS.ELA-Literacy.W.8.8), our students must:

Gather relevant information from multiple print and digital sources, using search terms effectively; assess the credibility and accuracy of each source; and quote or paraphrase the data and conclusions of others while avoiding plagiarism and following a standard format for citation.

Additionally, according to the Institute for Museum and Library Services website, our students must:

- **Use and manage information (information literacy)**: Apply a fundamental understanding of the ethical/legal issues surrounding the access and use of information.
- **Analyze media (media literacy)**: Apply a fundamental understanding of the ethical/legal issues surrounding the access and use of media.

In order to introduce ethical academic behavior, I first give my students a scavenger hunt of sorts through some resources in order to learn about my expectations. This launches further discussions that are ongoing with every writing assignment. Additionally, I continue to model what we've learned, and I hold them to the standards we've agreed upon.

I developed this scavenger hunt using Google Form, but you can just as easily do it in SurveyMonkey or Excel. You can see the whole assignment in Part II, page 142.

7 **Creating a Weebly site**: I have students create a Weebly site in order to house their creations as we progress through this unit. These websites reflect the individuals in each league; however, each student is responsible for producing his or her own page of the website as a means to get their message out to the public.

The superhero league website needs to have a number of elements before it can be declared complete:

- mission statement
- collaboration constitution
- page for each individual member
- research library page when members combined and listed all of their bibliographical research in proper MLA format.

8 **Creating infographics about your topic**: it's important to have students understand that text, numbers, and pictures have a relationship. Infographics not only blend them all, but also help to integrate subjects. For this unit, students design infographics about their selected topic as a means to help readers understand the urgency of the problem and the legitimacy of the proposed solution. I expose them to Piktochart.com as a great infographic-producing program, but I permit students to use any program to design their infographics so long as they include all the elements. Figure 1.5 shows one on the topic of Arson.

Homework Hint

Once you have introduced infographics to the students, have them find examples in the world outside of school and bring them in for credit. They can see for themselves that they need to understand how to read them if they begin to realize just how many are out there and how many subjects they represent.

Figure 1.5 Arson Infographic

9 **Drawing names for one's country**: it's important to note here that I didn't start the unit with this element in place. This part of the PBL unit was one that came to me while talking to myself in my rear view mirror on the way to school. Knowing that the bolt of lightening can come at any time, I prepped my students at the start of the unit to expect that the checklist was not set in stone. This element was added as the unit progressed and the strength of this addition to the project came more into focus.

Basically, it occurred to me that when the students presented as their superhero characters, the audience of students had nothing to do. This was unacceptable. So they became the ambassadors to the United Nations who had to question each presenter and evaluate which superhero's project to fund.

By having the audience role-play as well, it provided an additional layer of authenticity to our final production. These makeshift ambassadors made signs with their country's name complete with icons and symbols that represented their assigned country and conducted some independent research focusing on basic information about their represented nation.

What this did was prep the audience to listen to the advocacy speeches through the lens of what they knew about their country. In other words, if Mr. Inconspicuous (a masked hero one of my students created) presented on the dire need to fund a mythical organization dedicated to helping endangered animals, the speakers had to think about whether this issue was applicable to the needs of their assigned country. After all, they can't just fund every cause.

So we started by drawing names of UN countries out of a jar (see Figures 1.6 and 1.7) It's old school, but when jars come out, kids go nuts. I don't know why.

Homework Hint

Don't spend too much class time on the assignments for the ambassadors. Use homework assignments as a way to help them educate themselves on their assigned country. For instance, you can have them develop a document that lists the facts about the country, its main exports, the date it joined the United Nations, national flower, that sort of thing. You can also have students do a journal entry, using evidence and hyperlinks, that has them predict what issues that country might be facing and might want to see solutions to. This might help the student watch the superhero presentations though the lens of the needs of their assigned country. They are ambassadors, after all.

10 **Bringing in a subject matter expert**: with many PBL units, you want to try to bring a subject matter expert into the classroom. This can be an actual face-to-face interview or perhaps a Skype session. During this part of the unit, I actually was struggling with whom to bring into the classroom. Then it hit me: why not bring in the actual United Nations? To do so, we streamed live debate from the United Nations floor. There are also archives available that will allow you to download debates by date, so if you know when a particular debate came to the UN floor, search for it on their website. It was an effective day that really helped set the tone for the role-play to come.

Figure 1.6 Drawing Names from the Jar

Figure 1.7 Students Reading Their Country Names

11 **Advocacy speeches and oral presentation**: the end of the unit culminates in oral presentations and formal speech/essay writing. The students must use what they have learned throughout the semester to role-play as their superhero and present their findings to the ambassadors of the United Nations.

The format of their essay must be an executive summary. The outline of an executive summary can be found in Part II, page 144. For the purposes of this assessment, their essay and oral presentation had to include the following:

- different text structures
- hyperlinks
- a claim
- cited textual evidence form a variety of resources
- background information on the problem to prove its existence
- how it relates to their superhero
- a call to action that is concrete and specific as a means to solve the problem
- a logical prediction of the cost to solve the problem.

The format of their presentation is slightly different. The goal here is to create a vehicle to house all of their work and still cue students to present in a professional way without writing a script for themselves on the very slides we are looking at. That is, no blocks of text allowed on a presentation slide. The slides can be made using anything from Prezi to Google Presentation to Keynote to PowerPoint. The slideshow must include the following:

- at least 10 slides
- bullets only, no full sentences except for highlighting powerful quotations
- images on each slide

- ◆ the text should cue your speaking, not substitute for it
- ◆ data
- ◆ citation page at end
- ◆ cover slide
- ◆ background slide(s)
- ◆ evidence slides (s)
- ◆ call to action slide.

Oh, yeah. And the kids have to present in costume. See below.

12 **Teaching questioning**: meanwhile, the audience of students aren't sitting back and relaxing during the presentations. Nope. Remember, they are role-playing as well, as the ambassadors to the United Nations. While students are presenting, the UN will be on Google, typing questions onto a document as they think of them. It's all about assessing one's ability to question, and it's a digital version of Think Aloud.

I've written in the past about the importance of teaching how to ask questions. In my classroom, we speak the language of Costa. We talk about Level 1, 2, and 3 questions as those that prove their brain is activated. Asking students to ask high-level questions takes a certain level of scaffolding.

It starts small, with a mini-lesson earlier in the year defining Level 3 questions. From there, it's about providing students with the academic language they need to get them going. To do this, in the beginning of the semester, I displayed sentence stems to help them get started, but by the time these presentations had rolled around, I had taken down the scaffold. Then, depending on the assignment or unit, it's about giving them the format they need to contribute in an organized manner so they aren't just yelling out their questions in chaotic academic enthusiasm. In this case, I shared a document with my classes using Google Drive as a means for students to type in their questions publicly, in real time, as their fellow students presented.

We'd been using Google Drive all semester, so the students had a level of fluency using the technology. However, of all of the collaborative activities we did this semester, for whatever reason, these UN presentation days proved to be the most engaging and successful.

What I prepped ahead of time was a Google document for each period that had the list of presenters already entered in the order in which they were to present (see Figure 1.8). I used subheadings to divide them into dates.

Anyway, as students presented, I could watch as their questions lit up the Google doc. You could tell what presentations resonated or made the students really think because the high level questions were quicker to come. Controversial topics or solutions really made the doc go wild, and generally, as really great questions appeared, they would inspire students to revise their lower level questions or devise follow-ups to those already asked. In other words, the kids were learning from each other.

From there, I could look at my own monitor and announce the name of a country whose ambassador had a particularly interesting query for the presenter. The presenter would then say, "I recognize the delegate from Kazakhstan" or something like that. The student ambassador could then ask the question aloud and the presenter would try to respond using researched evidence.

The transparency of the document engaged everyone and encouraged the best from the students. I was playing along as "Heather (United States)," typing model questions along with them. By playing along, students who still struggled could take cues from my own questions and be inspired to ask their own.

In the end, many students who were normally quiet were encouraged by the ability to type their voice in class, and I had a chance to see them all think aloud through their real-time writing. Students were loosely scored on quantity of questions and the number of higher level (Level 2 or 3) questions.

It was great when the presenter answered these questions on the fly, but to be honest, that wasn't what I was assessing. Instead, I was assessing those who asked the questions.

It was a victory. It was a victory for Project Based Learning and for critical thinking using technology. Sure, when the whole class typed there was some lag. But the level of engagement kept kids patiently waiting when any glitch happened. It was a victory for flexibility, and it was a victory for higher level questioning.

A brief note about the power of backchanneling: this questioning activity was also a victory for the power of the backchannel conversation. Backchanneling is that second layer of discussion going on, a B-story as it were, that happens behind the scenes of a topic's main conversation. Twitter, as we know, is a program that allows people to backchannel. Todaysmeet is also a great, classroom-friendly backchannel program.

Figure 1.8 What Country Did You Get?

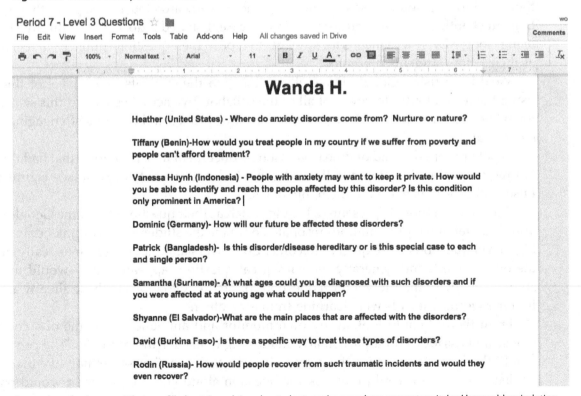

Screenshot of a document that was filled out, in real time, by students as the superhero presenter pitched her problem/solution.

However, to have a successful backchannel conversation going on simultaneously to other speakers presenting takes setting up norms early on. You can see the norms for backchanneling that I use in my classroom in Part II, page 145.

13 **End of unit survey**: at the end of any PBL unit, I conduct a survey of what worked and what didn't. This helps me to tweak the unit should I choose to do it again. It also tells me the impact it may or may not have had on the students themselves.

Figure 1.9 is my end of unit survey for my Superhero Unit:

Figure 1.9a, b, c, and d End of Semester Survey

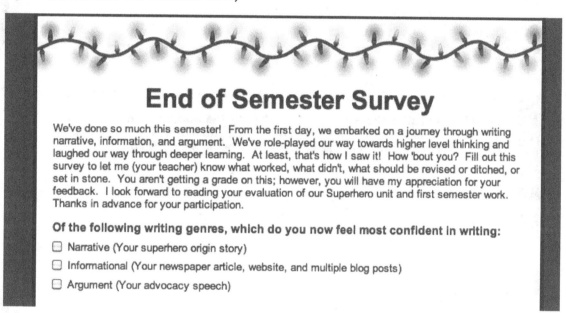

End of Semester Survey

We've done so much this semester! From the first day, we embarked on a journey through writing narrative, information, and argument. We've role-played our way towards higher level thinking and laughed our way through deeper learning. At least, that's how I saw it! How 'bout you? Fill out this survey to let me (your teacher) know what worked, what didn't, what should be revised or ditched, or set in stone. You aren't getting a grade on this; however, you will have my appreciation for your feedback. I look forward to reading your evaluation of our Superhero unit and first semester work. Thanks in advance for your participation.

Of the following writing genres, which do you now feel most confident in writing:

☐ Narrative (Your superhero origin story)

☐ Informational (Your newspaper article, website, and multiple blog posts)

☐ Argument (Your advocacy speech)

In terms of what you know about Multiple Intelligences and the use of many modalities in learning, what methods of learning and assessment did we utilize this semester?

☐ Visual (art)

☐ Linguistic (writing)

☐ Logical (numeracy)

☐ Interpersonal (working with others/collaboration)

☐ Intrapersonal (working independently)

☐ Kinesthetic (involving movement)

☐ Existentialist (studying theory and the big picture or vision)

☐ Musical (music, rhythm, rhyme, etc...)

☐ Option 9

(continued on the next page)

Figure 1.9a, b, c, and d continued

Of the following activities, assessments, and lessons, which of the following would you rate the MOST engaging?

☐ Origin Story
☐ Weebly Superhero League Website
☐ Newspaper article
☐ Collaboration Constitution
☐ Infographic Design
☐ Country Blog Post
☐ Advocacy Speech (written and oral presentation)
☐ Other: [   ]

Work load question: Rate your ability to handle the workload during this first semester. Think about this honestly. Assuming you didn't procrastinate, please rate your ability to keep up with the work that was being asked of you.

1 2 3 4 5

I couldn't handle the work load. Too much was asked. ○ ○ ○ ○ ○ I handled everything easily. No sweat.

Next Quarter: Shakespeare!

○ Can't wait!
○ Ugh.
○ We'll see...

Student Exemplars

After two intense quarters of narrative writing, advocacy speaking, and deep questioning, the students produced some great work and laughed a lot in the process. Figures 1.10–1.15 are just a few examples.

Collaboration Constitutions

Figure 1.10 Student-Created Collaboration Constitution

A.F.E. League Constitution
(Superhero Association for Fighting Evil)

Our League Objectives:
In the S.A.F.E. League our goal is to use our combined power and cooperation to protect the innocent people of the world from evil. Through fairness we hope to give everyone in this league a chance to rise up to their full potential for the well being of the group. We hope to give everyone a fair say in the decisions made by the league and an equal yet manageable amount of responsibilities within the league itself. Abiding the rules of this constitution we plan to save the world from evil at the best of our abilities as a team.

Roles of League Members
- Task Manager: Julia
- Typer-person: Alina
- Recorder: Stephanie
- Supplies Provider: Ciannah
- Timer/ meeting organizer: Kate

Rules of the League:
1. All league members must attempt to attend every group meetings.

2. Meetings will be held every one to two weeks.

3. Communication will be shared through email, Skype, or group texting.

4. 24–48 hours can pass before a response is considered unacceptable.

5. If a member of the league is not fulfilling their requirements the league will send a warning to the individual saying, "This league feels that you are not fulfilling your responsibilities as a member of the S.A.F.E. League and encourages you to get back to your work and finish it as soon as possible before we have to take a more serious approach on this issue."

(*continued on the next page*)

6. If a member of the league is not doing their work they will get three chances to complete it before the league will have to reevaluate their qualification for being in the league.

- First strike: Warning by email

- Second strike: Entire league talks with the person

- Third strike: Direct report to Mrs. Wolpert (unless there is a reasonable excuse)

Possible approaches to help a struggling group member:

a. Email/message them with a notice (should be agreed upon by the entire group)

b. Check their progress on their assigned share of the work (reminding, asking)

c. Giving them suggestions and feedback if they are stuck/ don't know how to move forward

7. The deadline for an assignment is one day before it is due into the International Organization of Supernatural Persons' President.

8. All roles and responsibilities assigned to a member of the league will remain the same through the duration of the league or until the role is reassigned.

9. Every meeting will begin with each member of the league stating their progress on their assigned responsibilities. Then details concerning the project as a whole can be discussed by all of the members. Finally any complaints, questions and clarifications can be dealt with before the next meeting is planned.

10. Everyone should give valuable input.
    a. Opposition to said input must be done academically and politely.
    b. Each member's opinions will always be considered.

11. All jobs concerning the members of the league should be assigned to fit their schedule and skills. If a member has an issue with an assignment they can contact the task manager.

League Motto

"Discipline yourself, and others won't have to."

Newspaper Articles

Figure 1.11 Red Reaper Newspaper Article

Limited Edition

Paper Lines

Issue 49 Vol. 17 | Monday, May 11, 1903 | 25¢

City in Ruins

CITY DESTROYED BY "RED REAPER"

Around 3 p.m. Sunday, a number of buildings were destroyed and burned down in the town of Darente, causing an estimated total amount of $100,000,000 worth in damages.

The destruction appeared to be the result of a fight between a fire magic user, dubbed "Red Reaper" by the populace, and members of a group who are currently pursuing her.

The reason why they fought is unknown.

Witnesses claim that the fight began in a restaurant in the middle of town, when multiple windows were suddenly shattered.

The subsequent fight enveloped the town and leveled whole buildings.

In the midst of the fight, however, the Red Reaper successfully escaped, and her whereabouts are currently unknown.

Amazingly, no bystanders were hurt in the crossfire.

The Red Reaper is described as a girl in her late teens, about 5 feet, 4 inches tall, wearing a red jacket, red pants, and an eyepatch over her left eye.

There was another person with her, a child about 12 or 13 years of age, whose relationship with her is unknown, though it is suspected that they are accomplices.

None of the people involved in the fight could not be reached for comment.

Red Reaper fighting with one of her pursuers, an ice manipulator.

AFTERMATH

Although no one was hurt, the citizens of Darente were badly shaken up by this event.

"First I was only worried about the destruction of our town," says Kielo Wilhelm, 26, who was working at the restaurant when the incident occured. "Now I'm worried about the world. You never know what someone like that can or will do."

For them, this was the first time they had experienced something like this. They had never gotten invloved in any of the conflicts that consumed the rest of the country before.

Even so, the people of Darente are slowly beginning to rebuild the shops and residences that were destroyed in the battle.

SEVEN DEADLY SINS

After that incident, some people began to believe that Red Reaper is actually one of the "Seven Deadly Sins."

All we know about the Seven Deadly Sins is that they are seven people who are possessed by demons, and each time the previous one dies, they are reborn as another person.

But whose fault is this?

Does this excuse Red Reaper from the destruction she caused, or does this just strengthen peoples' beliefs that "Red Reaper" should be locked away?

RED REAPER

A local artist at the restaurant at the time of the incident created a sketch of Red Reaper.

The govenment advises people to avoid anyone who resembles this dangerous criminal.

A reward is currently being offered for any information leading up to her capture.

A sketch of Red Reaper by a local artist.

Figure 1.12 Scarlet Mona Newspaper Article

Your Weekly Newspaper

Monificaus Valley Times

MV Junior High Student Causes Inexplicable Incident! Parents Demand Expulsion

By Rebecca Lin

Scarlett Mona, a seventh grader at MVJH, caused jaws to drop and parents to bombard school gates on March 24th due to her unexplainable use of what young witnesses claim to be "healing superpowers."

Mona was sitting alone on the school's football bleachers when Penny Mallory, one of her fellow classmates, fell off the bleachers and landed in an awkward position 18 feet below. When helped up by Mona, Mallory felt immediately recovered, clearly in a much healthier state than she should have been in after the fatal fall, according to onlookers.

Another similar incident bears testimony to the fact that this was not simply coincidental or a "lucky hit." Two weeks before, on March 9th, Mona had helped up her peer, Edward Hall, after he painfully lacerated his knees on the blacktop. Hall described his pain subsiding instantly "...like I had never or would never feel pain again."

Mona was rushed immediately to the principal's office where police questioned her before she was picked up by her legal guardian and sister, Codie Mona.

MVJH has agreed to suspend Mona for an undetermined length of time until enough parents and staff agree to let Mona back in.

Direct witnesses of Scarlett Mona's abnormal abilities were questioned this week along with several parents and Dr. Dave Gallagher, a physical scientist who has taken up on the matter.

When Mallory was questioned by the polic[e] and principal about her firsthand conta[ct] with Scarlett Mona, she admitted that sh[e] thought Mona was peculiar but had done [nothing] wrong. "...I don't think Scarlett should [be] expelled. She saved me from a lot of pa[in] my poor family from medical bills, and ev[en] [annoying] Eddie [Hall] from more bullyi[ng]. But I do think she isn't normal, either. It w[as] kind of weird and disturbing that I felt completely changed and mended after [she] had pulled me up." She says.

However, Penny Mallory's mother, [...] Mallory, has other words to say. "I — w[...] never! I say those cops should lock up [...] abnormal beast and leave her for [...] scientists to play with! I don't want my [...] associating with such unnatural people[...] though Penny says she feels great, I [...] her to be protected from the oddities [...] girl." Several other protective parents [...] similar comments to make about Sc[arlett's] apparent differences.

Dr. Dave Gallagher, who has ga[...] evidence and collected data in order [...] out more about Scarlett Mona's uncovered abilities, has come [...] conclusion that Mona is "...uniq[ue] extremely unusual; her actions s[...] explanation, and as far as scientific [...] this power has never been recorde[d]. Genetic wisdom of chiropractic [...] may play a part, but from wha[...] Mona's powers are a whole new [...] studies we must undergo to figure [...] says.

Photo: Gallag[her] School

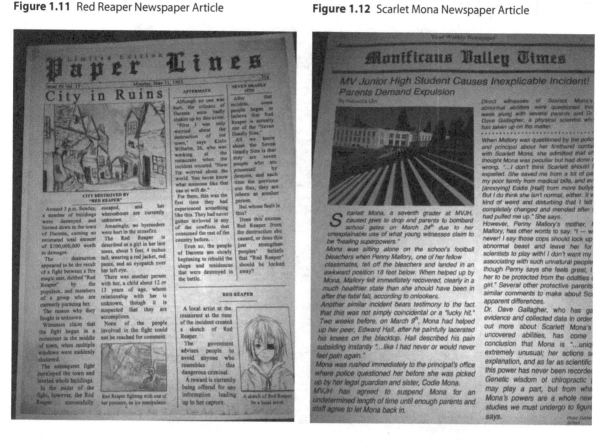

Presentation Pictures

Figure 1.13 Hugo as Livewire

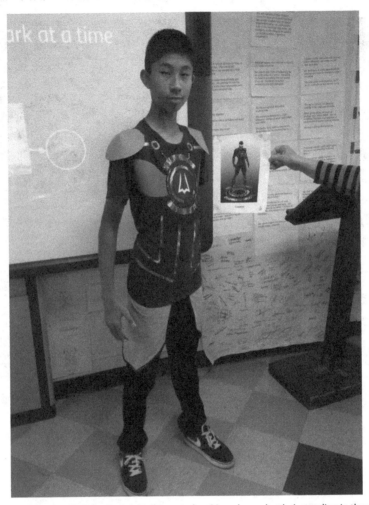

Notice that he not only designed the costume that he originally created on Marvel.com, but he's standing in the same position as the figure in the template. His topic was educating the world about renewable energy.

Figure 1.14 Christopher as Tidalwave

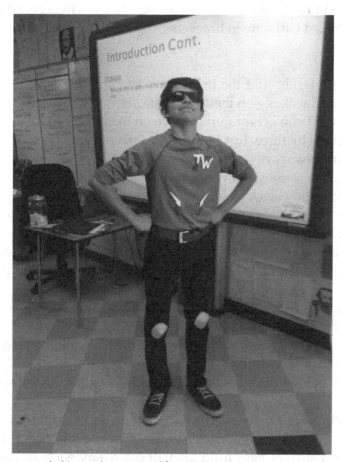

He used paper, tape, and iron-ons to make his superhero come to life to clean up the oceans.

Figure 1.15 Warren as Mechaman

He wore his tin foil epaulettes the whole day of his presentation. Clearly, he's enthused about presenting his infographic for the ambassadors to the United Nations assembled before him.

Origin Story

The underlined words indicate where the student chose to add a hyperlink to their informational research. The hyperlinked URLs are in brackets.

The Brash Beast

The sun was shining brightly, and the birds were singing; the three children of the Jackley family were content, and walking on their way back from school.

"Hey Jamie, what did you get for number two on the math quiz?"

"Pie times 50 divided by three. Just kidding! Jacob, you need to chill. Big bro, I'm sure you aced that quiz, like you always do."

"Will I ever receive a serious answer from you?" Jacob demanded as the trio rounded a street corner, on which a tiny black blob of fur rested.

"*Oh!* Look at that poor puppy! It's so cute! Can we keep it?" Julia interjected. She hopped up and down on her feet, pointing excitedly.

Jamie rolled his eyes, then glanced at the scruffy, black Labrador and laughed, "If we do adopt the dog, that probably means Jacob and I have to bathe, walk, and pick up after it right? No thanks!"

But Julia could not be beaten that easily. She used the single most powerful technique of persuasion a six-year old could possibly employ: she pouted.

"Oh please, please, pretty please?" Julia begged, and her smile widened as she witnessed her brothers' resolve weaken visibly.

"Well, I guess it wouldn't hurt if we fed it some food. Jamie, give it some of your leftover lunch," Jacob said.

"Why is my lunch the one being sacrificed? After all, Jacob, you have the most leftovers," Jamie replied seriously, with a grin that completely ruined the effect. He reached into his lunch bag, drew out a strip of ham from his half-eaten sandwich and approached the dog. As Jamie got closer, he noticed that the dog had begun to foam at the mouth [http://www.healthcommunities.com/rabies/symptoms.shtml], drooling green slobber. *Interesting . . . Isn't that supposed to mean something?* Jamie contemplated that for a second, staring at the dog [http://www.dogbreedinfo.com/articles/approachingdog.htm], consequently leading to the Labrador drawing his ears back and baring his teeth, growling and snarling suspiciously.

"Gee, you've had a bad day, huh? Here's something to make you feel bett—"

The dog snapped, then bolted away.

"*Ouch!*" Jamie pulled his hand back, surveying his bite wound [http://www.dogbitetreatment.net/]. The skin was broken, but he was bleeding a thick, smelly green liquid instead of blood.

Jacob and Julia rushed over to Jamie. "Are you okay?" both of them asked simultaneously.

"I guess I've been better," Jamie replied. He was feeling a bit dizzy and experiencing double-vision. Also, there was an excruciating pain at the back of his head, throbbing just as fast as his heartbeat. The throbbing intensified unbearably, and suddenly, Jamie was on the floor, clutching his hand.

Horrified, Jacob and Julia watched as fur began to grow all over Jamie's body. His face grew longer; his hands and feet morphed into paws.

A black Labrador puppy sat, wagging his tail and panting, clad in the absurdly oversized clothes of a 13-year-old boy named Jamie, who had stood there a few moments earlier.

Several seconds of stunned silence ensued, before the Labrador began to <u>writhe on the floor, and morphed</u> [http://www.wulfhowl.com/therianthrope-definition] back into Jamie.

"Do that again!" Julia cried.

"That was weird . . . It almost looked like . . .," Jacob continued slowly, ". . . you turned into a dog there for a second."

"Okay, perhaps we were just hallucinating, because the last time I checked, I was a human. Maybe if we give this whole thing a little while, we'll forget or it'll go away. Let's pretend it didn't happen, alright?" Jamie proposed. He was scared, but after all, maybe it would go away if everyone ignored it.

Jacob frowned, but Julia seemed to agree with the idea. "Yeah! Nothing bad will ever result if you just forget about it!"

All the way home, Jamie's mind kept returning to the dog's foaming mouth, no matter how many times he tried to forget it all. But of course, he didn't tell anyone.

The next several weeks passed by with no mention of that day. Jamie wouldn't have described the transformation as comfortable. However, he did kind of enjoy being a dog, even if only for 30 seconds. The ability to <u>smell</u> [http://www.pbs.org/wgbh/nova/nature/dogs-sense-of-smell.html] each and every flower, to <u>hear</u> [http://www.dogbreedinfo.com/articles/dogsenses.htm] a squirrel in the far-off trees; it was quite pleasant actually.

So one evening in his room, Jamie opened his science book and perused until he stumbled upon a page of animals. He stared intently at the first picture (a fluffy Maine Coon cat) and focused.

Yes! Jamie was an exact copy of the cat in the book. He spent some time frolicking and jumping on his bed before he wanted to try another animal. He closed his eyes, endured the same uncomfortable process of transformation, and became a human again.

Jamie looked at the next picture (a <u>Gray Bat</u>) [http://www.wildlifedepartment.com/wildlifemgmt/endangered/gray_bat.htm]. He stared intently and focused.

Nothing happened.

Well, maybe bats are too complicated. But then why was I able to turn into a cat?

Jamie morphed into a variety of animals: Labrador dogs, Siamese cats, pet hamsters, and parakeets. But he could never change into the <u>snow leopard</u> [http://snowleopardconservancy.org/kids/text/endangered.htm] perched on a cliff, the <u>lion</u> [http://www.fws.gov/endangered/what-we-do/african_lion.html] camouflaged in the grass, or the <u>elephant</u> [http://www.worldwildlife.org/species/african-elephant] at the watering hole. Disappointed, Jamie almost closed the book. But he noticed that all the animals he couldn't morph into had something into common: they were all under the title, "<u>Endangered</u>" [http://www.worldwildlife.org/species/directory?sort=extinction_status&direction=desc].

An endangered species? What does that mean? Jamie read the paragraph under the list. *A species whose numbers are so low, they are at risk of extinction.*

That's horrible! Jamie thought, as he pored over pages upon pages of illegal poaching and traps, of prized felts and ivory tusks. He couldn't believe the terrible things that humans did for greed. *Someone needs to do something, to save these animals.*

The Legend of Livewire

Bolts of lightning jumped from my hands like snakes hungry for food. They reached for anything that they could consume, which, at the moment, was everything. I watched in horror as bolts of lightning coursed through me and into the ground, igniting the dry, brittle hay that covered the floor of the barn. I spun around as the surges finally ceased. Flames licked the connector between the house and the barn. I tried to run to the house, warn my parents to get out, but a rafter dropped in front of me, just like in the movies. I cried out and jumped backward. I scrambled out of the barn, but flames continued to caress the house. My parents ran outside, and I could see that they were scared out of their wits. I caught something out of the corner of my eye, and I raced to get it away before . . . A mushroom cloud and dirty yellow flames shot up into the night sky, taking with them the people who had given me life. I hoarsely screamed my pain at the stars, tears blurring my vision. I wanted to give up right then and there, and throw myself into the flames that had taken my family, all I ever had, all I ever wanted. But I couldn't bring myself to. Then my parents' lives would have been in vain. What to do? I couldn't stay. Too many questions. I couldn't just leave my parents. I sobbed. I reached for a live wire, like an addict reaching for morphine. The tingling raced through me and into the ground. I didn't try to control it. The first sirens started to reach my ears. I ran to the woods like a wounded animal, seeking refuge.

I sat up quickly and banged my head on the shelf above my bed. The same flashback-dream, again, for the fifteenth time in a row. I sighed. Downstairs, my grandmother, La-Shonda, was making bacon and eggs, my favorite breakfast, for my first day of being a junior at LeBlanc High, in Chicago, or as it was more commonly known, Lehigh. I padded down the stairs and greeted my grandmother.

She was a great grandmother, who knew how to cook, when to help me, and when to stay out of things. I'd been living with her ever since I was six, when my parents died. So far, the only flaws I could find in her were that she slightly overcooked lasagna, and thought she still knew what "cool" was.

Before I walked out the door, I did what I do every day—check the matte black exoskeleton [http://www.techlife.net/2013/07/wearable-robots-powered-exoskeleton-provides-super human-strength.html] I'd started building in fifth grade. My favorite part was the helmet, for sure. In the front was a headlight that had four settings. On the left was a paper-thin electric thermometer, and on the right was a visor control that left my visor clear or tinted it black [http://science.howstuffworks.com/innovation/science-questions/question412.htm]. On both sides were audio microphones, and the edge above the visor held five different pinhole cameras. On the inside, tiny projectors displayed everything onto my visor, depending on whether it was clear or not. On the back was mounted the battery that powered the helmet. I'd designed it with lithium ion batteries [http://www.discovery.com/tv-shows/curiosity/] in each component, with electrical contacts [http://www.contacttechnologies.com/Contact-Technologies-Materials.htm] that touched my skin, eliminating the need for wires. That's right, I can conduct electricity [http://hyperphysics.phy-astr.gsu.edu/hbase/electric/conins.html]. From what I could tell from multiple blood tests and doctors' visits, I had an abnormally large amount of gold in my body, about 50 milligrams, rather than the usual 0.2 milligrams [http://www.gold-traders.co.uk/gold-information/how-much-gold-is-found-in-the-human-body.asp]. I also had extremely active electrical centers [http://www.biomedresearches.com/root/pages/researches/epilepsy/electrical_activity.html] in my brain, which contributed to the epilepsy [http://www.webmd.com/epilepsy/guide/types-epilepsy] that I'd had since I was 10. This gave me the power to channel electricity through my body, as well as control and produce small amounts of it, about 100 watts, enough to comfortably power a laptop computer [http://michaelbluejay.com/electricity/computers.html]. I could also feel emotions from people, and sometimes even strong thoughts, by "reading" the electrical signals of their brains. Sure, I guess you could say I'm a geek, but no one knew it, especially since I could beat anyone at basketball, and I never talked about it.

On the walk to school, I met up with my boys Jared O'Neil and Spencer Freeman. "Sup, DeShawn?" They exclaimed as they saw me. "Our little boy's gotten taller!" Yup, I was nearly the shortest boy in the school in 10th grade. That hadn't meant much at all, but after a summer, things were different. We walked to school together and shot the breeze.

At school, I was, as usual, one of the normal kids at the middle of the classroom, not answering questions until they were directed at me, but not like those kids at the back of the room shooting spitballs at the girls.

At lunch, I bussed my tray along the line and got the classic Monday meatloaf. I took the tray outside and immediately noticed the ring of kids on the basketball court, which always indicated either a fight or bullying. I asked Jared to watch my lunch, and I jogged toward the incident. I stayed out of fights, but bullying was just . . . not cool. As the circle broke to let me in, I saw my little cousin, Lil' Wilson, getting pummeled by—even worse—Sloan Aldrich.

"What, you want to die, just like your grampa did?" Sloan sneered at me.

My vision went red and I barreled into Sloan, knocking him sprawling into the blacktop. I distinctly remember pounding his face to a pulp, and people shouting for me to stop. What was worse, I remember fighting long after Sloan had given up. No one insulted my family, and especially not my parents and grandparents. Even my grandmother never talked about my deceased grandfather, Tyson Carter Jr.. But still, the power in my fists scared me.

I made it through the rest of the day okay, without any bullies or teachers or anyone getting mad at me, but not exactly with accolades. Walking home alone, I hoped that the dream I was having wasn't reminding me of that scene on purpose, warning me . . . Wait, what? I never walked home alone. I looked back, hoping to see Jared, my neighbor, straggling behind, but only saw the familiar stop sign. I shrugged and continued up the walkway to my house.

Unlocking the door, I was greeted warmly by . . . darkness? I didn't bother taking off my shoes as I went upstairs. I grabbed a few pieces of my armor, and put them on, on a hunch that I would need them, and I crept softly into my grandmother's room. I scanned the room, and saw my grandmother sitting in her favorite armchair . . . bound and gagged. I started toward her, but a man shimmered into existence behind her.

"What the . . ." I said something that might not be appropriate for me to say here.

"DeShawn Jones-Carter," the man drawled. His accent sounded weird, and I don't mean Russian, or Chinese, or anything like that. I meant weird like he wasn't from Earth, and was used to speaking in hisses, tongue clicks, and guttural noises. I guess that was a bad sign. I had no idea what could hurt this man, or help him. He was dressed like one of those gangsters from the 1920s, like Al Capone. I shimmered and disappeared, and I heard his voice behind me. I whirled around, and sure enough, I saw him there. I can't guarantee the lack of an expletive there, but I'm quite sure. I tried to run to my grandmother, but he reappeared halfway between us, then behind my grandmother again.

I raised my armor-clad right arm like I had done it hundreds of times before, and I suppose I had. I flexed my fingers, and the power glove [http://www.cnet.com/news/crush-enemy-bottles-with-this-power-glove/] I had on my hand responded perfectly, mimicking my every movement.

My instinct was to blast away, but my grandmother was in the way. I didn't want to kill her, and I didn't even know if I could electrocute [http://vias.org/feee/safety_04.html] this alien dude.

"Lower the weapon," he said, calmly. "I am not here on a violent mission. I am here to warn you of a coming danger, far more powerful than you or any other mortal can begin to fathom, to comprehend." That sounded both ridiculous and scary at the same time, sort of like the Silver Surfer from Fantastic Four. Any impending dangers except for a possible upcoming pop quiz seemed laughable.

"Will you join me and my people on our mission to save your planet?"

"Let me think about it . . ."

"No!"

". . . before I decide."

"You must choose now!"

I pondered the thought. This guy seemed like someone that I would want to be on the good side of. On the other hand, I wasn't sure I wanted to be caught in the middle of an alien war. I figured that I could do well by myself, here in Chicago. Maybe someday, when I was even more powerful, I would join the alien. Or maybe his race had a different sense of time, and what he foresaw would happen millennia in the future, when I was long gone.

"No thanks."

"Suit yourself," came the practical reply. "Farewell, human. It was a pleasure speaking with you." He shimmered again, then faded into nothing, like a dissipating mist.

I immediately leapt to my grandmother and untied the knots that held her tight to the armchair. I tucked her into bed and went up to my room to contemplate whether I had done something wrong, and if so, what. I decided to put off the strain and just try on the whole exoskeleton to see what would change in me as a person. Sure enough, as I put on the last piece, the helmet, I felt something click. Not in the suit, but in my persona. I finally felt at peace with the world, for the first time since my parents' death. I looked in the mirror and saw a daunting black figure, sleek, modern, and practical. I wanted a supername, that would finally make me whole.

In an instant, I had it. The perfect name for a guy like me. I was Livewire.

Advocacy Essays

The Brash Beast

Hello ladies and gentlemen! I have gathered you all here today (or maybe you've assembled here anyway) for a special mission. So listen closely! For those that don't know me, I am the Brash Beast. Now, as my power is the ability to change into different animals, I'd like to talk about a topic that's been plaguing my mind: animal testing [http://www.scu.edu/ethics/publications/iie/v1n3/cures.html]. More specifically, the lack of rules regarding it. First of all, you may be asking, "Ahem, Mr. Brash Beast, what *is* animal testing?" Well, animal testing/experimentation is the process of testing vaccines, medications, and procedures on animals, so that scientists may determine if they are safe for humans. It's sad, I agree, but a necessary albeit disheartening part of science. Through it, scientists are given opportunities to modify or change products, vaccines and other medications without a human ever being endangered. As a result, countless human lives have been saved. As current US Federal Law stands, all drugs have to be tested on animals before being distributed to humans. Like I said, sad but you can't break laws. Now, perhaps it's a little reassuring that the Animal Welfare Act (AWA) [https://awionline.org/content/animal-welfare-act], established in 1966 and last amended in 2008, dictates that animals used in testing and exhibition must be provided adequate food, water, and care. So the special mission that I have bestowed upon you, is to revise the AWA so that it covers all animal species, and also so that the fine for violating it is greater.

The AWA looks good on the outside, but in reality, it's not much. It only covers warm-blooded animals [http://animalrights.about.com/od/animallaw/a/AnimalWelfareAct.htm], so it excludes reptiles, fish, birds, and mice, even though those last two are warm-blooded. What's interesting is that those exempt species make up 95 percent of the animals used in experimentation. So that renders the AWA 95 percent useless as far as my topic is concerned. Our goal ladies and gentlemen, is to revise the AWA so that 100 percent of animals may be represented, protected from unnecessary harm, and entitled to humane treatment.

On to part dos . . . here's a thought provoking statistic: according to the Progress for Science Foundation, between 2010 and 2013 there have been 28 violations of the AWA [http://progress forscience.com/ucla2013violations/] in laboratories at University of California schools. Let me put this into perspective: in the course of three years, there have been 28 violations of the AWA. Of the AWA, that means that only animals covered by the AWA were inspected. Keep in mind the AWA only covers 5 percent of the animals used in testing. The universities that were cited for violations are not insignificant, run-of-the-mill schools: UC Davis, UC San Francisco, and UCLA contributed the most number of violations. These three schools are world-famous, and yet, they are not abiding by federal law. UCLA was charged with eight violations, from minor unprotected outlets to lying to federal authorities and refusing to let them enter laboratories. I believe the AWA needs to have heavier fines for violations; it's clear that the current penalties are not having an effect.

Volt

Correct me if I'm wrong, but there are 365 days in a year, right? Well, here's a hypothetical. Let's say that four children die every day [http://www.childhelp-usa.net/pages/statistics]. Hypothetically speaking, of course. But say that they do. Most people think that four is nothing. I mean, compared to the 17,119,871,679,229.42 dollars that America is in debt [http://www.brillig.com/debt_clock/] for, only four is almost laughable. But, what's 365 multiplied by four? 1,460. How about 10 years and four children die everyday? I'll let you do the math.

The thing is, I'm not speaking hypothetically. In America alone, four young kids have their lives ripped away from them by a monster, every single day. But the funny thing is that this monster is just a person, somebody like you and I. Hello everyone, I am Volt and today, I am putting a light on child abuse, a topic that has been pushed aside and neglected for no clear reason.

Many people believe that it is "only abuse if it's physical," but this is a huge misunderstanding. Child abuse can come in many different forms. Abuse can range from physical abuse, to emotional, and, most commonly, neglect [http://www.helpguide.org/articles/abuse/child-abuse-and-neglect.htm]. Anything that involves physically harming or injuring a child is considered as physical abuse. Meanwhile, there are many forms of emotional abuse. From downgrading a child to something as small as showing little to no affection can be deemed as being emotionally abusive. Neglect, which is the most common form of abuse, is simply not providing for a child's basic needs, such as food, clothing, and hygiene. All forms are heartbreaking because the young children we want to protect and nurture are being destroyed and corrupted by people they thought they could trust.

It is estimated that over 800,000 children are being affected both mentally and physically by abusive acts just in America. Worldwide, the numbers of abused children increase dramatically: 40 million [http://www.internationalcap.org/abuse_statistics.html] under the age of 15 are subject to abuse yearly. Take for example Minnesota Vikings' star running back <u>Adrian Peterson</u> [http://www.nydailynews.com/sports/football/peterson-leaves-vikings-critically-injured-son-report-article-1.1482734], who lost his two-year-old son due to a severe beating delivered by the mother's boyfriend, Joseph Patterson. <u>CNN News reports</u> [http://www.cnn.com/2013/10/21/us/adrian-peterson-son-death/] that Peterson's son faced serious head injuries that appeared compatible with abuse. The boy, whose name was not released, died in the hospital just a day after the attack.

Mr. Peterson's son was just one account of the thousands of children who are abused daily. Though only about four die on average daily, a report is made every 13 seconds, and though some attacks aren't as violent as others, the mental scarring is the same for every child. It is proven that in the US alone, children who were abused are shown to be nine times more likely to exhibit criminal behavior and about 34 percent of women in prison were abused mentally, physically, or sexually in their youth. Child abuse is also showing a correlation with substance abuse charges. <u>Childhelp USA</u> [http://www.childhelp-usa.net/pages/statistics] reports that two-thirds of drug addicts were said to have been abused during their childhoods.

In addition to these repercussions of abuse, <u>helpguide.org</u> [http://www.helpguide.org/articles/abuse/child-abuse-and-neglect.htm] reports other effects on the victims of abuse. These include feelings of being "damaged" or "worthless," as well as having lack of trust and trouble regulating their emotions. These <u>consequences</u> [http://www.prweb.com/releases/2013/4/prweb10673007.htm] can lead to depression, cancer, higher rates of heart disease, diabetes, and victims are more likely to die at younger ages.

Child abuse has plagued mankind for too long. Children are having their lives torn away from them by people who they believed were going to protect them; and though the solution seems simple, there is not enough manpower put into solving this epidemic. At the moment, the punishment for child abuse ranges only three months to 17.5 years and I don't know if it is just me, but that is not enough of a consequence for ruining a child's life. I propose that all the leaders of the world put their minds together and come up with a way to protect our children. I've tried to come up with a solution but my mind is not powerful enough to figure out a way to protect millions of children; however, I know that if we work together, put our differences aside, we will find a way to save and protect the future of our world because we are corrupting our children, our legacy, before our very eyes.

2

The Living Museum Unit

A unit based on role-play, historical perspectives, and informational writing culminating in a student-created living museum

Table 2.1 The Living Museum Unit Facts

Subjects Integrated	Writing: fictional memoir, informational
	History: Colonial America (or any other historical content area focus one can teach)
	Reading: informational and primary documents from first person POV
	Technology: hyperlinking, Google Drive, Garageband, collaborative mapping, etc.
	Art, music, acting
	Oral presentation and debate
Skills Used	Collaboration
	Problem solving
	Creativity
	Communication
	Questioning
	Role play
Duration	Approximately one month
Driving Question	How can we learn best from those who came before us?
	Or
	How can people make a difference in determining the tides of history?

Overview

Note: this unit is one of the earliest I ever developed. I worked with a remarkable team of teachers "back in the day," and every subject area teacher involved lent their area of expertise to the overall unit. The art teacher permitted us to use her time to develop backdrops that were historically accurate. The computer teacher worked with the students to develop elements of their arguments as well. In addition, my teacher partner at the time (in that school, we were lucky to have teams of teachers at each grade level) was a master in arts and working with recycled materials. I also learned a lot about teaching reading strategies with her. It should be noted that 15–20 years ago, much of what I was asking of the students tech-wise had to be taught, step-by-step. As time has moved on, however, I have found that students now come to me with certain things already known. In the unit below, I will scaffold it down to the main assignments and pacing of the unit, but read your students and know if you have to break down certain skills even further.

The purpose of this unit is to role-play as a villager in Colonial _____. Think about it like it's Williamsburg, but you can use your own school's name instead. Having said that, this unit could work *with any historical era*. Change the content they must learn, but keep the structure of the unit intact, and you can use it to debate any historical topic or simply to teach other classes in your school about your subject area. It is not limited to American History alone.

In the spirit of Project Based Learning, the Living Museum Unit uses the following elements:

- subject matter integration
- role playing
- oral presentation
- technology
- outside expert
- giving students authority over their learning
- student choice.

You can go one of two ways with the development of this unit, but you should know where you want the students to go ahead of time. Sure, you can do both, but that might be overkill for both the students and the school. Nevertheless, pick and choose from both goals what works for you, or simply focus on achieving one. Here are the two goals that you can choose to pursue:

1. The students will work to develop a living museum comprised of characters that they play. Each character is a villager in a mythical colonial town. The other classes in the school visit the museum and can walk around, hear the student monologues, and then ask questions of the villagers.
2. The students will role-play as villagers that must meet to debate a topic. In the case that follows, they are debating the Quartering Act and whether they should fight the requirement of housing soldiers in their homes. Other students from different classes can file in as audience to overhear the hushed "midnight" debate.

Step-by-Step Lessons

Table 2.2 Step-by-Step Lesson Organizer

Due Date	Assignment	On Time?
	Annotated research	
	Cornell notes	
	Character analysis	
	Journal assignment(s)	
	Home/shop visual for map	
	World cloud	
	Painted set piece	
	Political cartoon	
	Quartering act journal entry	
	Informational essay on trade	
	Memorized script for museum and/or debate	

1 **Create a timeline**: for this, students will use their historical resources to create a timeline of the era about which they are learning. There are many great programs out there to use, but you might want to give students the choice of the following:

- ◆ http://www.dipity.com/
- ◆ http://www.tiki-toki.com/
- ◆ https://www.timetoast.com/

This could be an individual long-term assignment or one in which the whole class can contribute.

2 **Teach students how to annotate their research**: regardless of the kind of text, students need to interact with their reading. Informational reading, such as that found in textbooks, many websites, and other resources, require students to mark up, highlight, and annotate. For a handout to help teach students how to interact with their material, see Part II, page 146.

Incidentally, teaching annotation helps hit many Common Core standards such as the goal to achieve certain levels of text complexity.

3 **Take a virtual tour of a historical facility that is relevant to your era**: if you are studying American history, check out the interactive Colonial Williamsburg website. You can look at the live streaming feeds from their webcams or even look at a map of the town. This is helpful because it can serve as a model for what will become your class's own interactive map.

4 **Pick a character**: have characters pick trades out of a hat (or, you can assign them if applicable). Don't spend time having students learn every single trade. Instead, have them focus on their own and then they can wander around the "town" and learn about others' as the unit progresses. It will create a deeper learning experience. www.history.org has a list that is a great place to start.

5 **Research the trade**: this is a great opportunity for an Internet literacy lesson that is appropriate for your age group. One such lesson might be to show students how to use Google Advanced Search. (Check out the lesson in Part II, page 133.)

Another great Internet literacy lesson would be one that focused on verifying the evidence in a Wikipedia entry. Wikipedia is a great place to start, but that's all it should be used for. It's a jumping off place. (Check out the Verifying the Evidence lesson in Part II, page 146.)

Make sure their research isn't just about what that person does, but also what their environment might look like. What could the interior of a smithy look like? What items would be on the shelves? What would be standing on the floor or hanging from the hooks on the walls?

6 **Cornell Notes**: have students take Cornell Notes as they research. Cornell Notes help students to organize their thoughts as they progress through higher-level reading. It asks them to develop questions, chunk their information, and in the end, to summarize what they've read. (To see a Cornell Note template, look in Part II, page 147.)

7 **Developing a character**: this lesson can be used for any narrative writing unit as well as this kind of role-playing unit. Basically, you are going to have the students create two characters. For each of them, have the students create a foursquare chart like the one in Table 2.3.

Table 2.3 Character Traits Chart

Name:

Age:

Theme/Motto:

Physical description	Personality
Goals, objectives, dreams . . .	What others say about this person

See a completed student sample on page 61.

Then, give them a prompt that might be an easy debate of some kind. It can be historical in nature given the era about which you are studying, but it should be easy. For this lesson, you are merely working on written voice, not research. The point is to have the student write a back-and-forth discussion between these two characters, focusing on the differences between the written voices of the two. The student will then select the character he or she wants to "be" for the remainder of the unit.

Homework Hint

Have students write journal entries in the voice of their character throughout this unit.

---

8 **Teacher-created map**: as a prep for the next part of this unit, find a topography map that reflects the environment in which a colonial town may have been placed. Try to find one that has a waterway of some kind, perhaps hills on one side, etc. It should be varied enough that students must make decisions when selecting the location of their home and place of business.

The map itself can be one that rolls out onto a table in the classroom, or it can be digital from the start, but eventually, you will be recreating it online so students can hyperlink their work to each of their locations. For instance, if a person clicks on the apothecary's shop, a student's essay will open up so allow readers to learn more about that character's trade.

9 **Creating the town**: once students are familiar with the needs of their trade, have them come up, one-by-one, and select the location for their shop. This will also help determine the roads and where the center of town will need to be located. Students will hand draw (and then scan) or digitally create their shop icons and labels.

This collaborative map will also serve, in a way, as a Museum Directory, helping the audience to see the diversity of the trades in the room as well as the depth of research involved in creating the living exhibit.

10 **Create the interior of each shop**: we gathered refrigerator boxes for a while, and then cut them into tall triptych-like backdrops that the students then painted as interiors of their shops or homes. This takes a while, but once the research is done, the students can sketch it all out on the cardboard in pencil within one class period or so. From there, the painting is done within free time once other work is completed. Make a deadline so students can then choose to work on these during lunches or recess if necessary as well.

You can also probably do this kind of activity with something less freestanding, such as rolled up poster paper. Or, if you are really innovative and have access to multiple projectors, the students can create something digital that is thrown up on the wall behind them. Me? I'm all about the cardboard.

11 **Declaration of Independence word cloud**: I'm nuts about word clouds. They are visual ways for students to clearly see the main idea about a particular document. In this case, have the students use Wordle or Tagxedo to create a cloud that gives them access to some of the most common words found in a key document from the era. This isn't just a pretty project, however; this is going to help them develop the oral and written language that will be a part of their role-play in front of their audience.

Once the word cloud is created, have them develop a list of 10–20 words, perhaps the words that appear the most frequently in the primary document (see Figure 2.1). These words can then be used in the development of their own Declaration of Independence or when writing and speaking on their historical topics.

Figure 2.1 Declaration of Independence Tagxedo

12 **Political cartoons**: one of the first political cartoons was Benjamin Franklin's "Join or Die," published in 1754. Have students study political cartoons and create one of their own, based on a topic from the time period. For instance, if you wish your students have a public debate, perhaps have the students create a cartoon about the side of the debate in which they stand. Or, if you want more variety of topics, give them a list of Acts that were being debated at that time. A great way to start is to introduce students to symbols that might represent different concepts. Of course, there are always students who are comfortable with stick figures too. See Figure 2.2 for an elementary-level example (it would have been a better example if the person sleeping in the bed were actually wearing red, however).

Figure 2.2 The Quartering Act Political Cartoon

13 **Student-created debate script**: if you are going to have the students recreate a public debate, you need them to memorize a script. To create a collaborative script using the voices of the student characters, give them a final journal prompt on the topic of the debate. Have them do a timed write that must include the following:

◆ a strong stance on one side of the debate or the other
◆ word choice that reflects the period
◆ written voice that reflects their character
◆ dates and facts that led up to their position (textual evidence).

Gather these journals together and create a script from the lines written in the journals. Create a back-and-forth using the opinions and sentences that the students wrote themselves. Keep track of which student wrote which line and these will determine who is speaking when.

Another variation of this would be to create a Google Document that all students can add to in the voice of his or her character. The only drawback here is that some voices will dominate and others might not add. One can also create a discussion post of the debate prompt and assign students to comment in the voices of the characters. This too will give you the fuel for the final student-created (teacher-edited) script.

Figures 2.3–2.5 show student samples of journal entries. From there, cut and paste key lines to create the back-and-forth debate.

Figure 2.3 Student Journal Entry

July 8th, 1765

For the first time in 8 years I feared for Sir Graham; Sir Grahams allowed british soldiers into his home, and when they entered they immediately asked for food and drinks. Sir Grahams forbade me from even offering them even the slightest amount of corn mush, much less serving them one of our valuable pigs. They threatened Sir Graham by telling him that he would be arrested and put to death for not acting in correspondence of the Quartering Act. Dame Grahams (the wife of Sir Grahams) then pleaded with them not to arrest him, and then ordered me to begin preparing a grand dinner for the soldiers. I immediately started preparing our largest pig and began cooking apple pies. I was careful to make sure to use the freshest ingredients. I usually only cook for two people but now I must cook for 5 under short notice. I had no help from, Azah a slave that works on Sir Graham's plantation; she is an amazing cook. As I was cooking, the british soldiers came into the kitchen and began to take ingredients that I was using and began to eat them. The fresh apples I planned on using for my pie disappeared after 5 minutes.

When I finally manage to pull together a dinner of corn mush, roasted pig, fruit, and molasses, I prepared 7 plates; 5 for the soldiers and 2 for the Grahams. I brought the plates to the table and to my surprise only the soldiers sat in the dining room table. I served them, and let me tell you, I have never been so offended in my life. If I wasn't a proper lady I would have told those lonesome toads that they were natural cowards without instinct. I wanted nothing more than to be better strangers with these men. They began to tell me that the food they had in their mouths was foul, and it probably was considering they had eaten all my fresh ingredients.

After the dinner I gracefully prepared was somewhat eaten they then left the house. I then proceeded up the stairs to Sir Graham's rooms to alert them that the british soldiers had left. With this news Sir Graham began to scorn me for not following his instructions. According to him I was instructed not to give the soldiers a morsel of food and that I should never listen to his wife's instruction because she does not own my contract; but the kind Dame Graham excused me for the day and sent me to my small room I had in the attic. Never have I ever been faced with such such ungrateful lœches.

This Quartering Act demands that us the colonist provide for the british soldiers. I already owe Captain Broadbent hundreds of pounds already and after one more month my contract with Sir Grahams will be completed and I then will have to repay the captain in full. I now must provide for ungrateful swine and repay my debt. If this continue my one bright future will be cut short. I refuse to continue with this act.

–Lunete Yoxall

Figure 2.4 Student Journal Entry

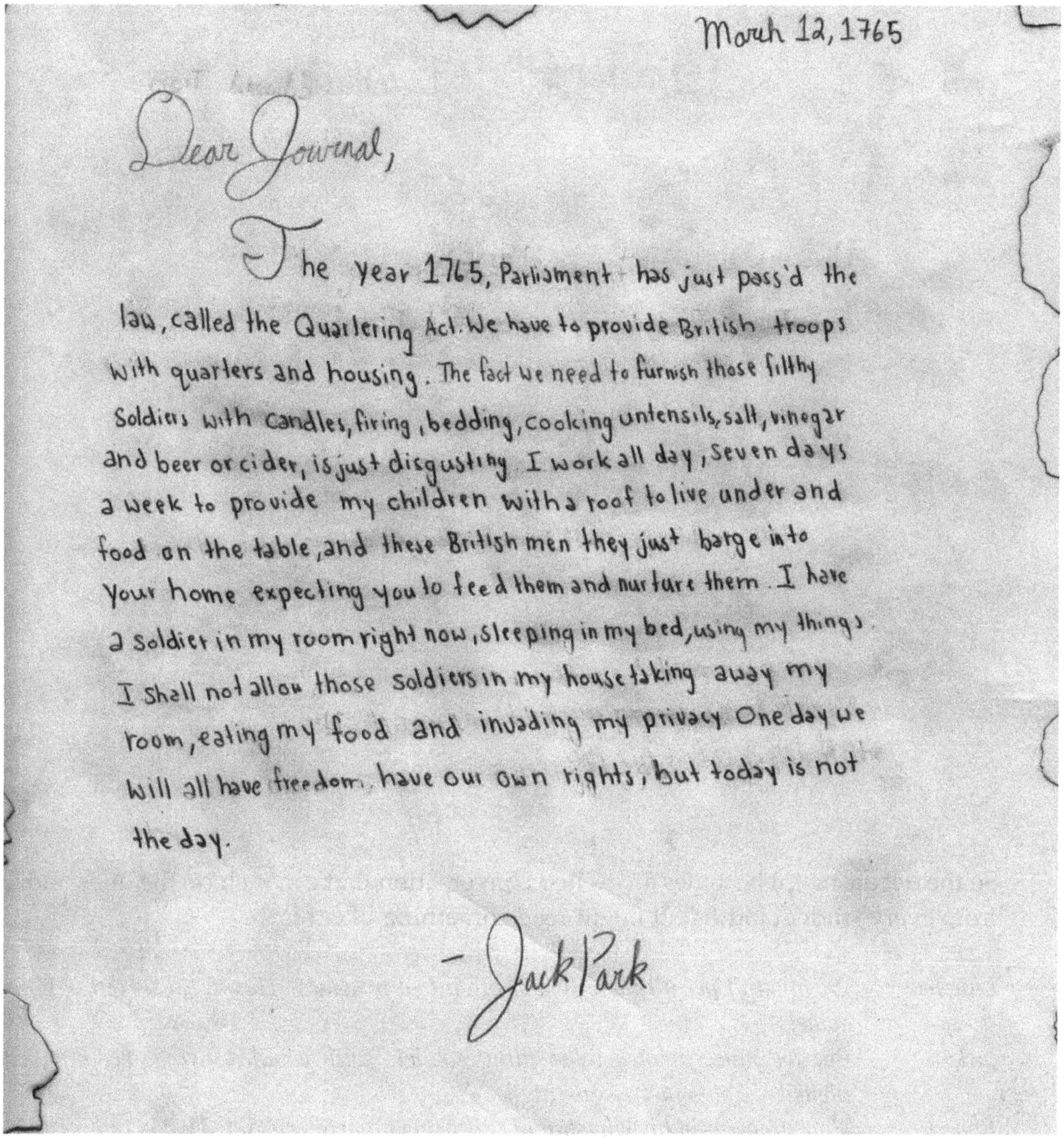

March 12, 1765

Dear Journal,

The year 1765, Parliament has just pass'd the law, called the Quartering Act. We have to provide British troops with quarters and housing. The fact we need to furnish those filthy Soldiers with candles, firing, bedding, cooking untensils, salt, vinegar and beer or cider, is just disgusting. I work all day, seven days a week to provide my children with a roof to live under and food on the table, and these British men they just barge into your home expecting you to feed them and nurture them. I have a soldier in my room right now, sleeping in my bed, using my things. I shall not allow those soldiers in my house taking away my room, eating my food and invading my privacy. One day we will all have freedom, have our own rights, but today is not the day.

— Jack Park

Figure 2.5 Student Journal Entry

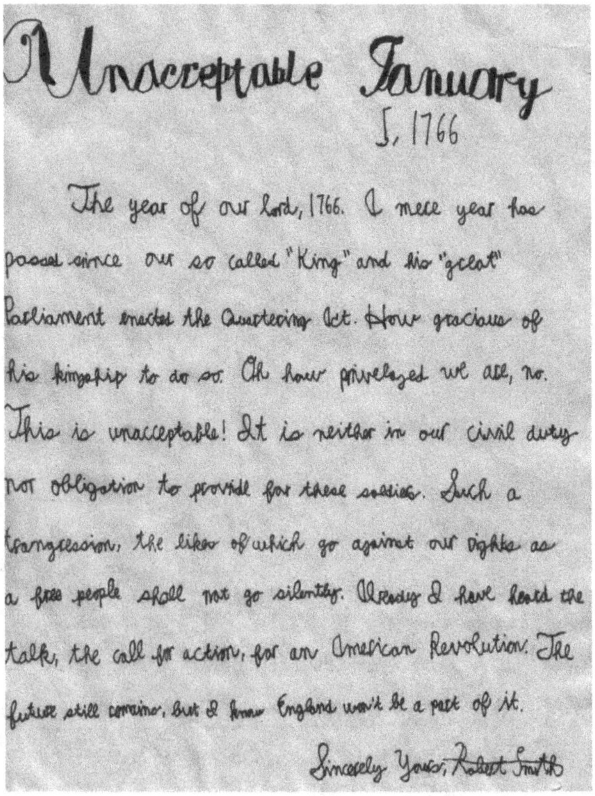

Unacceptable January 5, 1766

The year of our lord, 1766. A mere year has passed since our so called "King" and his "great" Parliament enacted the Quartering Act. How gracious of his kingship to do so. Oh how privileged we are, no. This is unacceptable! It is neither in our civil duty nor obligation to provide for these soldiers. Such a transgression, the likes of which go against our rights as a free people shall not go silently. Already I have heard the talk, the call for action, for an American Revolution. The future still remains, but I know England won't be a part of it.

Sincerely Yours, ~~Robert Smith~~

So the debate script becomes an excited conversation that can include the lines and voices from every student journal. It might read something like this:

Lunete:	*We mustn't permit these Red Coats into our homes! They'll eat us out of house and home!*
Jack:	*But we must furnish those filthy soldiers with candles, firing, bedding, cooking utensils . . . it's just disgusting.*
Robert:	*How gracious of his kingship to enact this Quartering Act. This is unacceptable!*
Jack:	*I, for one, shall not allow those soldiers in my house, taking my room, eating my food, and invading my privacy!*
Lunete:	*But The Quartering Act demands that we colonists provide for these British soldiers.*
Robert:	*It is neither our civic duty nor obligation to provide for these soldiers! Such transgression, the likes of which go against our rights as a free people, shall not go silently. Already I have heard the talk, the call to action, for an American Revolution.*

14 **Informational writing essay**: have students write an essay that teaches their audience about their trade. Have facts throughout the essay that are hyperlinked to external and credible websites that show the students' agility with both primary and secondary resources. The essay itself will be hyperlinked to the image of their shop/home on the interactive map at the entrance of the "museum."

In terms of the Common Core standards, this hits many, including:

CCSS.ELA-LITERACY.RH.6-8.1
Cite specific textual evidence to support analysis of primary and secondary sources.

CCSS.ELA-LITERACY.RH.6-8.2
Determine the central ideas or information of a primary or secondary source; provide an accurate summary of the source distinct from prior knowledge or opinions.

15 **Costumes for the museum**: make sure that students look their part. Maybe a parent can step up and help them create their tri-corn hats, but everything else can be found in closets and drawers around the house. Tin foil buckles are awesome. Long socks pulled up with sweats tucked in at the knees keeps up the colonial appearance. There's no need to buy anything so much as simply plan ahead and keep looking around before the deadline.

16 **Establish norms for your audience**: have the students create a list that they would like their audience to follow. Brainstorm as a class and then create a collaborative document that students can add to. Format this as a poster in the front of the museum or as a handout by the door.

One list my students created included the following:

1. Show respect *(Note: I followed up on this suggestion with the question: What does respectful look like?)*:
   ◆ sit facing the speaker
   ◆ make eye contact and nod
   ◆ ask questions that follow-up on what was said.
2. Laptops at 45 degrees if we aren't actively typing our notes.
3. Only use G-rated language (PG maybe).
4. Don't interrupt.
5. Use evidence, cite sources, and show your research when you ask questions.

17 **Museum day**: OK, the kids have worked hard and the day is upon you. Have the students stand in front of their stores and answer questions as other classes walk around during scheduled times throughout the day.

If you are doing the debate component, it might be nice to set up a different kind of atmosphere. The year we did that, we put all the boxes together in a ring and turned out the lights in the multipurpose room in order to give the appearance that the villagers were meeting in secret in a local barn to debate the Quartering Act. The audience sat on the floor surrounded by the villagers, who had rehearsed the script in hushed tones. The final moment was broken up when a student playing a Red Coat busted through the cardboard "door" and broke up the meeting.

Student Exemplars

Figure 2.6 Colonial Character Analysis

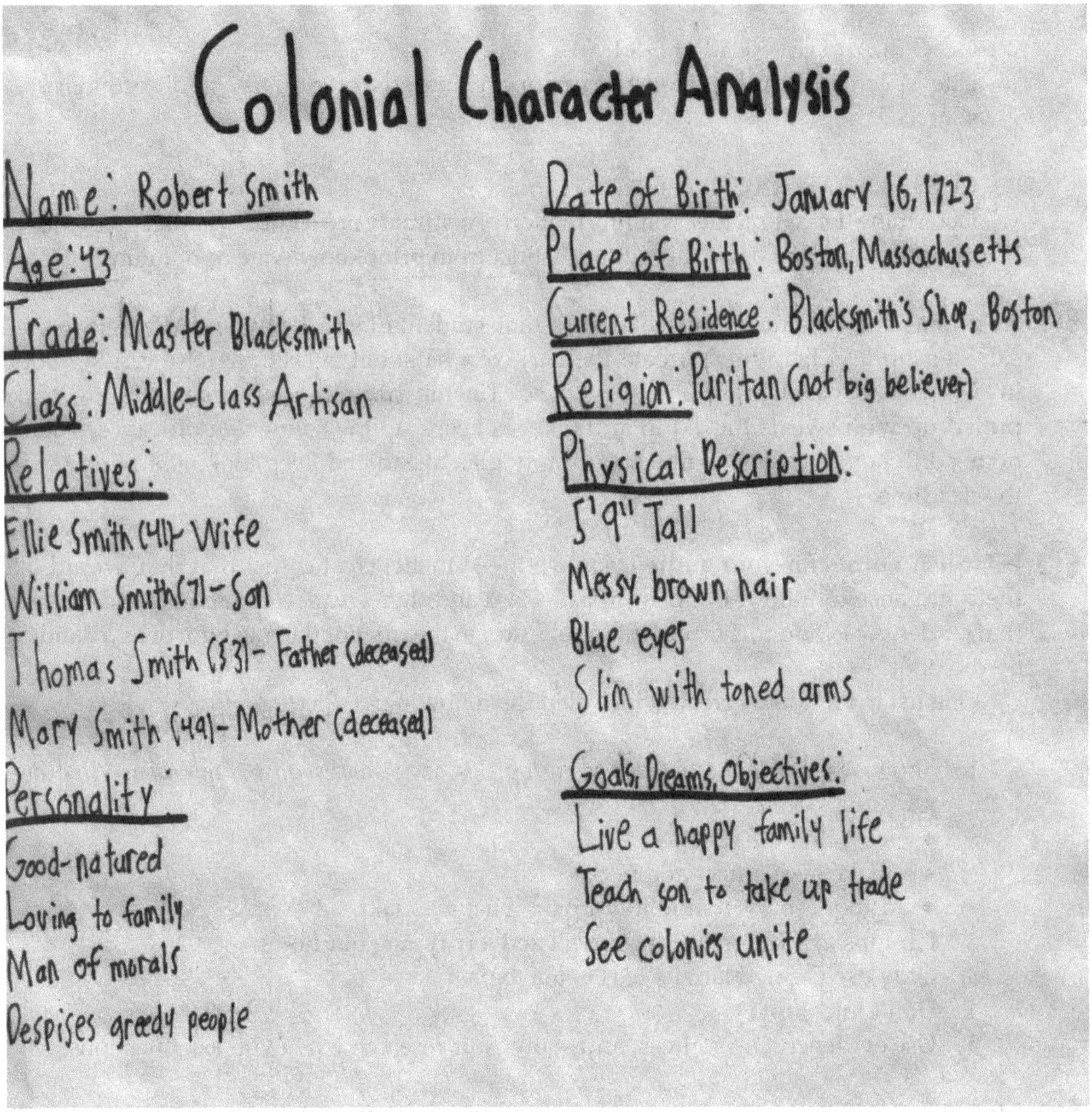

Colonial Character Analysis

Name: Robert Smith

Age: 43

Trade: Master Blacksmith

Class: Middle-Class Artisan

Relatives:

Ellie Smith (41)- Wife

William Smith(7)- Son

Thomas Smith (53)- Father (deceased)

Mary Smith (49)- Mother (deceased)

Personality:

Good-natured

Loving to family

Man of morals

Despises greedy people

Date of Birth: January 16, 1723

Place of Birth: Boston, Massachusetts

Current Residence: Blacksmith's Shop, Boston

Religion: Puritan (not big believer)

Physical Description:

5'9" Tall

Messy, brown hair

Blue eyes

Slim with toned arms

Goals, Dreams, Objectives:

Live a happy family life

Teach son to take up trade

See colonies unite

Figure 2.7 Colonial Character Analysis

Name: Evan Park

Age: 39 years-old

Trade: Silversmith: makes things out of silver

Class: middle class

Background: Born on November 13, 1726. Lives with family: wife and 2 kids.

Physical Descriptions	Personality
• apron • spectacles • curly brown hair • beard and mustache • tall • black boots • Green and Blue eyes • Dirty clothes • Broad Shoulders • muscles	• Family first • Loving • persistent • Stubborn • Smart • clever • rebellious • clumsy
Goals, Dreams, Objective	What others say
• move to a higher class. • kids grow up and do something better. • The Quartering Act would end. • rebell against the Quartering Act. • the world would be peaceful, full of freedom and rights.	• He's such a great person • I agree that we should not have The Quartering Act. • He's generous and knows what's right and wrong. • He's very clumsy tipping over water, but he's still a nice person.

3

The Movie Critic Unit

A unit based on literary analysis, biography, and film appreciation culminating in a persuasive argument and student-taught lesson

Table 3.1 The Movie Critic Unit Facts

Subjects Integrated	Writing: literary analysis, argument
	Reading: informational, drama
	Technology: Twitter, word processing, Internet literacy for research, Google Drive, hyperlinking
	Film appreciation
	Theater: scene study
Skills Used	Collaboration
	Creativity
	Communication
	Critical thinking
	Oral presentation
Duration	Two weeks–one month
Driving Question	Is everyone a critic?

Overview

This unit explores the many authentic ways in which people are constantly using analysis during their 21st-century daily lives. Let's face it, Literary Analysis or Response to Literature is one of the more inauthentic writing genres that students are asked to produce. It is difficult for students to recognize analysis in the real world. However, when you talk about reviews for books, music, or movies, then their eyes light up and they understand perfectly that "everyone's a critic."

During this unit, students will explore the world of movie critics as those who analyze for a living. They will develop different products that use analysis in order to portray a narrative, namely those used by movie industries. Then, students will focus on the contributions and life of the late movie critic, Roger Ebert. Finally, students will analyze their peers' scene studies through the professional lens of being movie critics themselves.

I should note that while my unit is done in conjunction with the end of a small group scene study from William Shakespeare's A Midsummer Night's Dream, the fact is that you can have the students "critique" any kind of medium.

The unit begins with an overview of many different kinds of reviews and then focuses more specifically on movie reviews as model texts for the kids' own literary analyses. After studying reviews, writing reviews, and even tweeting reviews, students will then transfer their knowledge of analysis to the real world outside of school. This unit culminates in a collaborative list of book recommendations and corresponding reviews created and donated to their local library.

This unit covers many of the elements of PBL by including the following:

◆ subject matter experts brought into the classroom
◆ curriculum integration
◆ collaboration
◆ multi-media resources
◆ community service
◆ role play

Step-by-Step Lessons

Table 3.2 Step-by-Step Lesson Organizer

Date Assigned	Assignment	How to Submit/Deadline
	Why do we study literature: short answer essay	
	Goal-setting	
	Literary analysis rough draft	
	Evidence vs. commentary: C.P.R. activity	
	Movie poster literary analysis	
	Guest speaker notes	
	"At the Movies" flipped homework assignment	
	Roger Ebert blog post analysis	
	Scene study	
	Microblogging Twitter/Todaysmeet activity	
	"At the Movies" partner transcripts for literary analysis	
	Literary argument essay	
	Google poll	
	Teaching peers to write an analysis: student-developed lesson	

1 **Why do we discuss literature?** It's important that you, the teacher, acknowledge that the excitement in discussing and analyzing literature should not be confused with the boring humdrum that is writing the five-paragraph essay about literature. It's not surprising that many people, our students included, merge the two, finally deciding that discussing literature is as pointless as the format we've been asking them to write all these years. They deserve an explanation. Kids these days deserve to know why they must do things in school; and, no, "because it's on the test" doesn't cut it.

To combat this, I begin the analysis unit with some kind of discussion and written response on the purpose of analysis.

Why Do We Discuss Literature?

Literary Analysis can be a difficult genre to learn because many people believe it doesn't exist in the world beyond school. I would beg to differ, however. We are constantly analyzing everything we see and read and hear every day. In terms of analyzing literature, however, there are many theories.

Read the following Time Magazine article.

http://ideas.time.com/2013/06/03/why-we-should-read-literature/print/

According to the article, why is it important to read and discuss literature? Going one step further, what do you see as the value in reading and discussing books?

In a one- to three-paragraph response, describe your experiences discussing literature: what's worked, what hasn't, and what you have gotten out of different experiences. Be as concrete as possible. In this case, your evidence is your memory.

Submit it by the end of class.

Homework Hint

Have students write a short Quickwrite on the following topic: What do critics do? What do they assume is the job of a critic? This can be used as an exit card or an introduction to a class activity on the topic.

2 **Show students some model texts from critics**: see my initial assignment as follows.

Even though we study literature and presumably we've just completed reading a common book (in my case, I do this unit after my students have all read William Shakespeare's A Midsummer Night's Dream) the fact is that analyzing a book is not so different than analyzing any other medium.

In fact, there are those who do this sort of thing for a living. They are called critics. Being a critic actually requires that you blend writing genres and create, in a sense, a persuasive literary analysis. They use textual evidence to convince us of their opinion or interpretation. The initial challenge, of course, is to find model texts. It's hard because Literary Analysis doesn't exist truly except in school. But if I look at it through the lens of "critic," it opens up a whole world of analyses texts to share.

Check out these posts that I think can be used as literary analysis models. Then, search online for your own models and share them with us here. Provide a link or file and then give your rationale for selecting the piece as a model text.

CNN Blog: "Ron Weasley, One of Us" (http://geekout.blogs.cnn.com/2011/11/04/ron-weasley-one-of-us/)

CNN Entertainment: "What exactly is 'The Hunger Games?' "(http://www.cnn.com/2011/09/29/showbiz/movies/hunger-games-craze/)

NPR recording of Kenneth Turan's LA Times review: "Borrowers' Tiny World Comes Alive in Arrietty" (http://www.npr.org/2012/02/17/147024270/borrowers-tiny-world-comes-alive-in-arrietty)

Don't limit yourself to literature-based analysis. Just think on what's out there in the world beyond school. Check out what's being reviewed on the red carpet, what critics are saying about a newly-released movie or music track, etc. Think "outside the box" with literary analysis and we just might crack an otherwise inauthentic nut.

3 **Setting goals**: as with many units, I begin with students reflecting on their previous relationship with a writing genre. In this case, the students set goals about the elements of literary analysis with which they still struggle (they are 8th graders who have written this genre enough to know what elements of writing still plague them). Their choices will help guide my new seating chart. I want them to sit with people who have listed their challenges as one of their strengths.

4 **Literary analysis outline**: of course, although I believe that outlines are scaffolds that shouldn't be used as the end-all-be-all structure of essay writing, we all know that there are still students who need those scaffolds. For this reason, I've provided an outline in Part II, page 148 that you can use with those students who still need the cueing for their ideas to take shape.

5 **Writing a literary analysis rough draft**: OK, you might think I'm crazy, but I believe that after showing students some model critiques, you can now send them off to actually try writing their own analysis based on a book you've read in your own classroom. In this case, I'm assigning one based on William Shakespeare's A Midsummer Night's Dream. However, you can use any book or short story to achieve this goal.

In this case, the point is to get something substantial on the paper or into the computer so that we have something to massage and revise as the unit progresses. This rough draft is, therefore, not to be graded. It is more of a formal, independent brainstorm that will lead into their final Literary Analysis that will be due at the end of the unit.

Literary Analysis in the Real World

Follow the directions below to learn more about literary analysis in the real world.

Go to Amazon and look at the reviews for Divergent (http://www.amazon.com/Divergent-Veronica-Roth/dp/0062024035). These reviews are written by people like you. The best ones go into detail about the story, what's great or what's not, character traits, and even themes. The reviewers bring in evidence from the book to make their points.

Then go to the New York Times and read their review (http://www.nytimes.com/2011/05/15/books/review/young-adult-books-divergent-by-veronica-roth.html?_r=1&). This was written by a professional journalist, and also uses summary, evidence, character information, etc.

Now imagine . . .

You are a writer for the New York Times Book Review. A play has landed on your desk that needs to be reviewed for that Sunday edition of the New York Times. It is William Shakespeare's A Midsummer Night's Dream.

> Your assignment is to write a book review of AMND. The following must be included:
>
> Title, Author, Genre (TAG)
> Brief summary (two to three sentences only)
> Your opinion of the book
> Textual evidence (quotes)
> Commentary
> Character traits
> Theme
> Conflict
> Setting
>
> **This assignment should be a page in length (at least) and is due on Thursday, March 13 at 11:59pm.**

6 **Evidence vs. commentary**: so now you've seen what your students are capable of in terms of writing a literary analysis. Let's be frank: the essays stink. Look them over and see what skills need to be highlighted and what mini-lessons need to be developed that can meet those writing gaps that you see.

Chances are, however, if you are teaching anybody aged 8–88, it's the commentary that's lacking. Students, for the most part, know that they need textual evidence. Many of them know how to pull quotes to prove their claim. But then what do they say about it? It's hard for humans of so little experience, who have just not been on this planet for very long, to construct commentary. They struggle sometimes with thinking about their own thinking. So I've devised a little acronym to help scaffold teaching commentary.

After all, the commentary is where all the fun is. That's where being the critic comes in. That's where students get to dirty their hands a little more, sharing their original thoughts and ideas regarding the quotes they've pulled and/or the ideas they've presented.

In my last book, *Writing Behind Every Door: Teaching Common Core Writing in The Content Areas*, I wrote about what I call the CPR strategy of writing commentary:

> I always tell students that a piece of writing, even informational writing, without commentary is flat and dull. They need to inflate it with their thoughts. I call it giving an essay CPR. To trigger commentary, I give them the following choices:
>
> C – Connect to Self, the world, the media, etc.: where have you seen this evidence before?
> P – Predict: what would happen if . . .?
> R – Relate the evidence to a metaphor or commentary: what does the evidence remind you of?
>
> There are other choices too that just don't fit into the nifty acronym:

Q – Questioning: can you develop a high level question to ask about the evidence?

E – Evaluation: what is your opinion of the evidence you found?

Homework Hint

There are a number of assignments that help students practice developing commentary, no matter the subject matter. One of the assignments asks students to comment in different ways based on a given claim (see Table 3.3).

Figure 3.1 shows one based on a scientific principle presumably used as textual evidence:

Figure 3.1 Commentary Practice

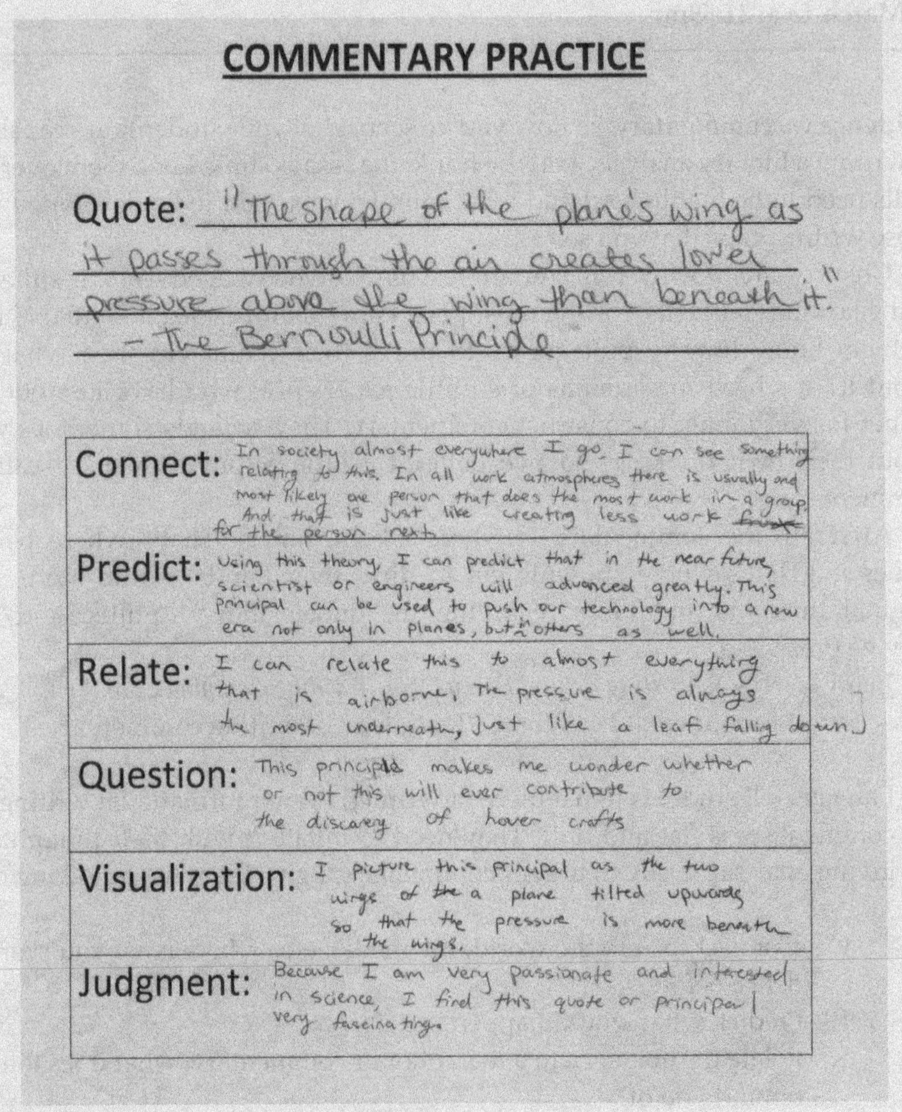

COMMENTARY PRACTICE

Quote: "The shape of the plane's wing as it passes through the air creates lower pressure above the wing than beneath it." — The Bernoulli Principle

Connect:	In society almost everywhere I go, I can see something relating to this. In all work atmospheres there is usually and most likely one person that does the most work in a group. And that is just like creating less work for the person next.
Predict:	Using this theory, I can predict that in the near future, scientist or engineers will advanced greatly. This principal can be used to push our technology into a new era not only in planes, but others as well.
Relate:	I can relate this to almost everything that is airborne. The pressure is always the most underneath, just like a leaf falling down.
Question:	This principle makes me wonder whether or not this will ever contribute to the discovery of hover crafts
Visualization:	I picture this principal as the two wings of the a plane tilted upwards so that the pressure is more beneath the wings.
Judgment:	Because I am very passionate and interested in science, I find this quote or principal very fascinating.

Here's one based on a history-based statement:

Evidence: "The right of citizens of the United States to vote shall not be denied or abridged by the United States or any State on account of race, color, or previous condition of servitude" (The Bill of Rights).

Table 3.3 Sample Homework Assignment

Connect	This makes me think of Martin Luther King's legacy and the rights that he fought for.
Predict	I predict that different cultures and races will use this right to balance out and unite the U.S. We can divide easily as a result of our differences, but the fact that we aren't restricted from voting due to skin color connects us together.
Relate	This people of the U.S. are like the colors of the spectrum. We're different but when we, as colors, come together, we become one.
Question	Why isn't gender included in this quote?
Visualization	I visualize a blind person managing the voting booths. They don't see color or race when allowing someone to vote.

Specifically covering the difference between Evidence (cited facts and/or quoted contributions by others) and Commentary (the author's original thoughts and contributions to the essays) hits the Common Core standards in many ways. For instance, it hits:

CCSS.ELA-LITERACY.W.8.1.B
Support claim(s) with logical reasoning and relevant evidence, using accurate, credible sources and demonstrating an understanding of the topic or text.

7 **Movie posters and movie trailers as Literary Analyses**: OK, so students have read a book or short story, and you've gone over it with them. They've read some reviews as model texts. They've even written a rough draft of an analysis. However, now it's time to ask the question, do analyses have to happen through essay writing?

The answer, of course, is no. So in keeping with the theme of this unit, students are going to explore movie posters and movie trailers as a means to analyze and pitch.

The movie poster: what makes a movie poster an analysis, you might ask. Well, let's look at one together. If you look, for instance, at the movie poster for 2012's blockbuster smash, The Avengers, you'll see that you learn a lot about the movie just by analyzing the poster. Go to www.imdb.com for a clear image of the poster.

Some discussion points:

1. You'll notice that many movie posters work in layers of three. That is, there is a foreground, a background, and a layer of images in the middle. Ask students the following:
   - ◆ Using literary terms, what images make up the foreground? (*The main characters*)
   - ◆ What images make up the middle layer? (*New York*)
   - ◆ What images make up the very background? (*The cloudy sky with exploding spaceships*)

2. What do you notice about the proportions of the main characters? Can you tell main from minor characters?

3. What about the cityscape gives you the impression that this is a science-fiction genre?

4. What are the characters standing on? What does this indicate about the plot of the movie?

5. Now, let's look at the credits. Who wrote the movie? Who directed the movie? Who did the score/music? Did someone do two jobs on this film? Can you predict or hypothesize something based on what you know about multitasking?

6. Many movie posters have a slug line, a single sentence or phrase that captures the tone or the gist of the movie and is meant to draw a viewer in to buy tickets. The Avengers doesn't have one, but what would it be if it did? For this one, I always give the example of my favorite poster line of all time from the classic Nicolas Cage virtuoso, Valley Girl. I still remember it to this day: "She's good. He's hot. She's from the valley. He's not." Brilliant. I bought a ticket as soon as my mom dropped me off at the mall.

As a mini-project for students to show their understanding about movie poster design, they will be asked to create one themselves. While I allow students to use any medium with which they are comfortable (Word, Photoshop, Illustrator, markers and crayons, etc.), I introduce them to a simple poster creator that can be found at http://bighugelabs.com/poster.php.

The student must design one based on the book we've read, and it must include the following:

◆ a slogan
◆ an image that describes character or conflict, tone or plot
◆ credits
◆ preferably layered images if the program allows.

See some student samples on page 78.

Additionally, students are asked to work in small groups to create quick book trailers to promote A Midsummer Night's Dream. We generally use the iPads in the classroom with the iMovie app, but many students also go off on their own and use Windows Movie Maker or even Animoto.

There are many great examples of model book trailers out there. Here are just a few:

◆ Shiver, by Maggie Stiefvater: https://www.youtube.com/watch?v=QX82ggGCF7c
◆ Going West, by Maurice Gee: https://www.youtube.com/watch?v=F_jyXJTlrH0#t=75
◆ Tell Me a Secret, by Holly Cupala: https://www.youtube.com/watch?v=HqzUuoAmTJs#t=48
◆ Matched, by Allie Condie: https://www.youtube.com/watch?v=xaeNWL8rlBI
◆ The Clockwork Angel, by Cassandra Clare: https://www.youtube.com/watch?v=tntndQF4eV0#t=43

Ask students what the purpose of the movie or book trailer would be. From there, have them watch the model trailers to identify their common elements. After that, it's simple to assign students the job of creating a book trailer. Make sure you donate some class time to this assignment, but students should also be working on this at home. Remember, as with any small group activity, always have the students draw up a Collaboration Contract ahead of time (see page 37 for an example from a prior unit).

8 **Subject matter expert**: at this point, I brought in a subject matter expert—my dad. My dad writes screenplays for a living and he knows a thing or two about critics. Now, I know you may not have your own personal screenwriter, but it's important to tap into any experts you may know to lend their expertise to the students. Do you know a journalist? Do you know an author? Can your students write letters reaching out to any of the critics they've read from the model pieces you've examined?

Don't worry if you don't have someone to bring in at this stage, just look through the unit overall and see who you can tap to highlight a particular skill or lesson.

9 **Meanwhile, the kids are readying their scenes**: remember that this unit began as one that allows us to interact more closely with a text. In your classroom, perhaps you've read Thank You, M'am. Maybe you've read The Outsiders. Maybe you're even a math teacher having assigned Flatland. Have the students who worked together on their book trailers work together again on developing a particular scene to perform for the class. These scenes should be memorized and blocked by the students themselves. Give them some in-class time to work, but also let them know you expect them to work independently as well. Also, prepare them for the fact that they will be performing in front of professional critics.

Now we have to teach them how to critique like the pros.

Homework Hint

Because my unit was centered on Shakespeare's play, I chose to have the students watch an excerpt from Gene Siskal's and Roger Ebert's show, At the Movies, that reviewed what would become the Best Picture Oscar-winning movie from 1998, Shakespeare in Love.

I flip the assignment a bit here and ask them to watch the footage at home. You can find it here:

http://www.youtube.com/watch?v=pVUHF7xLBwk

Then, I email them a five-question Google Form to fill out before midnight as a little piece of evidence that they did the assignment.

---

10 **Introduction to Roger Ebert**: after they see At the Movies on their own and answer the questions, I then watch it again with them, adding my own commentary. However, since they have already presumably watched it, they can jump into the discussion with more informed gusto. We then move on to studying Ebert's writing as critical analysis.

I introduce this lesson as follows.

You have been working as actors and directors for these past couple of weeks. We, as students, have also been studying analysis. These two go hand-in-hand. When a person analyzes an art form, such as theater, music, books, or movies, you are actually acting as a critic of sorts. You aren't a critic that takes joy in tearing apart a piece that someone has worked on and denigrating it. No. You are a critic because you like to tease something apart and **appreciate** its components.

Let's also appreciate someone who worked to give professional critics a place both at the computer and in front of the camera: Roger Ebert.

Last night, you were to have watched Siskel and Ebert's review/analysis of Shakespeare in Love, the Best Picture Oscar-winning film from 1998. I have the results of your Google Form that shows me what you understood from the video. Today, we are going to look at a written version of a Roger Ebert review, this one from his blog post criticism of 2002's Spirited Away:

http://www.rogerebert.com/reviews/great-movie-spirited-away-2002

Let's look at the blog post together and think about the elements of literary analysis.

1. What is the statement, the clear claim that gives Ebert's main topic or purpose of the essay? Write it here.

_____

_____

2. Write one piece of textual evidence (a quote) that Ebert includes in the post to prove a point that he is making.

_____

_____

3. Does he give some kind of background or summary of the movie for those who may not know anything about the topic? Y/N

4. What kinds of Commentary do you see in the post? Circle all that apply.

Prediction
Opinion/Evaluation
Question
Connection to something else
Relating something to a metaphor or simile
Visualization

⓫ **The life and times of Roger Ebert**: during this unit, the students also learn about what made the man. Roger Ebert was a great critic in part because of his brain, but also because of his heart. That's what made so many actually listen to him, even as he criticized their work. Along those lines, we look as his biography: http://www.biography.com/people/roger-ebert-554976#awesm=~oAXcwiqPhCwx1G

As you can tell if you've looked at this website, Robert Ebert's image on the homepage is vastly different to the one from the youtube video. His illness and learning of his recent death has an impact on the kids. In fact, after his death, an article from The New York Times wrote the following:

> Roger was not one to collect disciples, but he taught a lot of us—and I don't mean only, or primarily, professional critics—a lot of what we know about movies and about criticism. It's hard work, but anyone can do it. All you need are eyes, a voice and a friend in the next chair to tell you when you're wrong.

Because of his life and career, a recent documentary has been produced about his contributions as a critic. At the time of writing this book, the movie hadn't yet been released. However, I used other supplemental artifacts to enhance the resources for the students, for example the trailer for the movie and articles such as this one from the New York Times: http://www.nytimes.com/2014/06/29/movies/roger-ebert-is-remembered-in-the-documentary-8216life-itself8217.html?_r=0.

12 **Scene study analysis**: throughout these last few weeks, the students have been working on their scenes from the books that they have read. These need to be ready to be performed in time for the opportunity that follows.

In terms of quality of presentation, I spend some time talking about blocking, setting, character portrayal, etc. Focusing on the interpretation, after all, is an indication of comprehension. In addition, I do a one-day mini-lesson on stage combat. Remember, we've been focusing on A Midsummer Night's Dream, so this is appropriate for our purposes. However, I think the important takeaway here is that it's great to get the kids outside and moving every once in a while. They'll thank you for it later on with their enthusiasm for whatever you throw at them next.

I also have a green screen in the classroom. Nope, I don't show them how to use it. I don't fully know myself. But the minute I brought it into the classroom, kids asked to fool around with it, and as a result, they began exploring with different settings and stagings of any pre-recorded scenes. Give students a list of days on which groups will be performing so that it's not a mystery.

I score the final scenes on a 1–5 rubric. I go over the criteria ahead of time so there aren't any surprises. Table 3.4 shows the rubric.

Table 3.4 Scene Study Rubric Template

Criteria	Actor #1	Actor #2	Actor #3	Actor #4
Visuals: costumes, props, etc.				
Volume				
Connecting to fellow actors				
Preparedness (memorized if applicable)				
Attempts at character				
Overall cohesion				

Total score:

A rubric that is filled out might look like Table 3.5:

Table 3.5 Sample Scene Study Rubric

Criteria	Actor #1	Actor #2	Actor #3	Actor #4
Visuals: costumes, props, etc.	5	4	5	5
Volume	4	4	4	3
Connecting to fellow actors	4	3	4	4
Preparedness (memorized if applicable)	5	5	5	2
Attempts at character	5	5	5	4
Overall cohesion	5	5	5	5
Total score:	28/30	26/30	28/30	23/30

The students will be pretty busy ramping up to their performance, but remember, in this PBL unit, they are working as audience members as well.

13 **Microblogging—Twitter as a form of critique**: when the students are audience, you will also be asking them to interact with the experience by tweeting out their opinions of what they are seeing.

Twitter, at its basic core, is a form of analysis, but its power to capture the gist, the nugget, of a meaning is huge.

The goal of microblogging, as one does with Twitter, is to have students practice using analysis under a character limitation. This pushes them to get to the point of their criticism with as much efficiency as possible.

Before you launch into Twitter or any other microblogging program, however, make sure that you work on building the community in your classroom. Critiquing takes a subtle and steady hand or it can become mean. Students need to be soaked in an environment of professional behavior and appropriate feedback. What I mean is that this can't be the first time the students have given feedback to one another. This is merely another method to do so.

I would also suggest showing them what microblogging is in an offline form first. That way, they can more fully wrap their heads around the concept of Twitter as analysis.

Once you have decided, however, to use microblogging with your classroom community, also make sure you go over the Norms of Backchanneling (see Part II, page 145). Better yet, develop those norms yourself with the students' input. They will certainly own the rules far deeper that way.

However, because of the age of the students and the nature of criticism, we aren't going to use Twitter as our microblogging program. Instead, we are going to use Todaysmeet. Todaysmeet allows a teacher to open a Twitter-esque room, designate a name for that room, distribute it to students so that only those students can participate in that feed, and close the room as soon as the activity is done. It's a closed-campus, Twitter environment. Additionally, students have to use their login name so that they aren't tweeting anonymously, and teachers can print out the whole transcription when it's done for record-keeping or display purposes. Just go to Todaysmeet.com to begin your secure microblogging activity.

Once you have gone over the concept of analysis set to the tune of Todaysmeet, introduce them to their purpose.

I say the following:

As an audience member, you will be a movie critic. Recently, you have been working in a small group, developing a chosen scene from A Midsummer Night's Dream. But when you are the audience, you have another job to do as well. You will be pretending that you, like Roger Ebert, are watching students' scenes from a mythical balcony in a movie theater, and "tweeting" about your analysis.

Before we begin to tweet ourselves, however, let's look at some of Roger Ebert's tweets and examine the quality of his 140-character analyses.

After his show was cancelled in 2010, Ebert took to social media with his love of movie analysis. After his death, his wife, Chaz, continued his feed. Figure 3.2 shows examples of tweets made regarding movie reviews:

Figure 3.2 Roger Ebert's Tweets

Your job is to be a movie critic of an upcoming cinematic adaptation of A Midsummer Night's Dream (the scenes that you and your fellow students will be performing in class). Imagine that you are in a special screening room that will allow you to tweet your analysis of the scene in real time while also seeing the tweets of those around you.

Using the standard tweet structure of 140 characters or less, you will analyze the scenes as they are being performed (or just in the five minutes after each performance). Each critic is being asked to contribute at least one **positive** observation to the online conversation. The Todaysmeet room will be closed after the period is over. Each "critic" will be scored on participating in this micro-analysis.

Think about the elements of analysis and commentary. Make sure that your tweet has an element of analysis within its 140 characters: show-off your knowledge of narrative, of format, of character, conflict, director's choices, visual choices, etc. but keep it professional. You may also add external links as you feel they are needed.

From a critic's point of view, have fun. Enjoy being entertained as much as Roger Ebert did.

Here are some examples from that activity. These are transcribed from the Todaysmeet feed itself.

> Love Helena! She uses her height so well to make her point! Frenemies until the very end!

> Leo makes a great Demetrius. He and Kevin really worked on the Nerf swordfighting choreography! #TOLO (thou only live-est once!)

> Puck seems to really keep one foot in the fairy's world and one foot interacting with the audience. Shakespeare uses him to pull us in.

> I wish Hermia & Helena were more choreographed. By standing separated on two sides of the room, the audience didn't get the tension as much.

14 **At the Movies Literary Analysis**: once students have explored the different formats analysis can take (posters, trailers, tweets, blogs, and articles), it's time to ask them to write their own formal literary analyses. However, we still want to keep this authentic. To do so, they are going to role-play once again as critics, this time as Roger Ebert and Gene Siskel from At the Movies.

Have students pair up. If possible, pair them with some kind of a recording device as well, something that will capture their voices—faces aren't necessary for this activity unless they want to further the role-play. Have them simply discuss the book that they will be analyzing, trading off time to speak so that it isn't an argument so much as a discussion that mimics the At the Movie format.

From there, have the students build their formal essays using transcriptions of their discussions. This helps them by allowing discussion prior to writing as well as giving them access to another student's brainstorm as well. They can, therefore, construct their essays using information from either partner or both of them.

Inevitably, students will come to the conclusion that there is an element of persuasion in analysis; to which you should reply, "Bingo."

Under the Common Core standards and according to any authentic example of literary analysis, formal responding to literature has a new relationship to argumentation. Literary Analysis comes in many forms, and we all struggle to find authentic models to make this genre meaningful. The Common Core spins Literary Analysis in an interesting way: use it as argumentation. In other words, convince the reader of what you know about literature. After all, argumentation is a universal genre that is found in every discipline.

This new Literary Argument then helps us launch into the culminating chapter of this unit: critics for the community.

15 **Critics for the community**: the goal for this segment of the unit is to use our literary analysis expertise to benefit our local community. Students will be looking at lists of Top 100 things of all time and then, as a class, designing their own list of recommendations to share with their local library.

Homework Hint

Give them resources such as the AFI movie list: http://www.afi.com/100years/ movies10.aspx. Ask them to identify those they have seen. Of the ones they have seen, ask why they think it made the list? What elements of the movie might be seen as such high quality?

16 **Top 100 books of all time**: this is when we transition from talking about movies to talking about books.

The students will examine the Time Magazine and BBC "Top 100 Books of All Time" memes. These will serve as models for our own list, called "Top ___ Books Every Middle Schooler Should Have Read by the End of 8th Grade." Insert your own grade level there.

17 **Literary argument essays**: students will write arguments to justify why certain books should be included on our list. These arguments will help seed our all-school poll. (See the argument outline in Part II, page 148.)

18 **All-school poll**: once the arguments were produced, I developed a Google Form that was a survey of all the books mentioned. At lunchtime, we set up tables with Chromebooks that allowed the whole school to trickle in to vote on the books that they felt were the most important to read. So, let's say there was a list of 100 to choose from. You can give students the option to select around 50 of them. The ones with the most votes get a place on the list that will eventually be submitted and posted by the local library in time to give advice to students for their summer reading lists.

Homework Hint

Have students produce promotional posters to hang around the lunchtime stands that advertise the books they would most want to see win a place on the list.

19 **Preparing the library list**: the final list that is produced for the library should include a table made up of the title, author, and genre of the books being recommended. There should also be a column that includes an awesome quote from a student's essay describing the book itself. The list should be in order from 1 to 100 and should be mounted on a poster or printed in a book that should be displayed at the front of the children's section of your local library. This way, their ability to analyze will have been used to advise others of what to read next.

20 **Follow-up role-play as teacher**: at the end of the unit, depending on time, the students will have to design a lesson for the class to teach the skill that they first listed as their most challenging when writing analysis. After all, "whoever does the teaching is doing the learning." See Chapter 6, The Teach Them to Be Teachers Unit, for ideas on how students can develop lessons to teach their peers.

Student Exemplars

Figure 3.3 A Midsummer Night's Dream Movie Poster

Figure 3.4 *A* Midsummer Night's Dream Movie Poster

The Career Quest Unit

A unit based on persuasive cover letters, developing resumes, interview skills, culminating in a school-wide Career Day event

Table 4.1 Career Quest Unit Facts

Subjects Integrated	Writing: informational, persuasive, cover letters, resumes, emails
	Reading: informational
	Technology: Google Drive, emailing, video conferencing, website building
	Oral presentation/interview
	Community service
Skills Used	Collaboration
	Problem solving
	Creativity
	Communication
	Role play
	Etiquette online and face-to-face
Duration	Approximately one month
Driving Question	How can we leverage our passions into careers? How can we invest in ourselves?

Overview

The Career Quest unit is based on developing the aptitude to pitch oneself. The students role-play as interviewees for a particular position, and as a result, work on persuasive writing, oral speaking skills, and website design. When we talk about college and career readiness, we aren't necessarily talking about prepping students to learn to create the actual resume and cover letter for the job for which they will definitively apply. The role-play here is meant to push students to begin thinking about their own passions in a more career-oriented way, and to learn how to leverage those interests in an academic manner.

During the unit, the students will be applying for wacky jobs that utilize their strengths as defined by the students themselves. The students will develop digital portfolios that will pitch their skills to a formal audience. They will also have a three-minute oral presentation in the format of a prepped "job interview" with the teacher or outside volunteer expert who will stand in as the role of possible "employer."

By the end of the unit, students will be writing letters asking community members from outside of education to participate in a student-run Career Day for their school. This community service will bring experts into the classrooms and educate all students on college and career readiness.

In accordance to PBL, the Career Quest unit uses the following elements:

◆ subject matter integration
◆ role playing
◆ oral presentation
◆ technology
◆ outside expert
◆ college and career studies
◆ student choice
◆ multi-genre writing
◆ informational reading and writing.

Step-by-Step Lessons

Table 4.2 Step-by-Step Lesson Organizer

Due Date	Assignment	Stamp	On Time	Late
	Reflection chart			
	Personal research design			
	Cornell notes			
	Works cited /bibliography of research			
	Recipe of a job well done			
	Flow chart of pathway of study to pursue the career			
	Biography/informational essay			
	Cover letter rough draft			
	Wanted ad journal entries			
	Business card rough draft			
	Interview questions written responses			
	Final draft resume and final draft student choice cover letter			
	Digital portfolio			
	Interview oral presentation			
	Business letter invitation			
	Thank you letter			

1 **Reflection chart:** the unit begins with the student thinking deeply about what they like to do and what they are good at. These can sometimes be different things, but the goal is to help them tease apart their strengths so that they can see just how varied and "pitchable" they are.

Have the class create the table shown as follows, four columns in size. Model your own detailed brainstorm. For instance, Table 4.3 shows the start of my chart.

Table 4.3 Student Reflection Chart

What I Enjoy Doing	What I'm Good At	What I've Been Paid to Do	What I Do That I'm Not Paid For
Talking about Shakespeare	Doodling	Teaching	Making dinner
Watching movies	Character voices	Typing	Cleaning the kitchen
Reading sci-fi books	Talking about Shakespeare	Wrangler at a dude ranch	AYSO Team mom
Cooking	Making kids laugh	Babysitting	Reading picture books
Thanksgiving dinner	Reading	Publicity Dept. at a studio	
Teaching teachers		Filing	
Studying biology		Flipping burgers	
		Librarian	

The students want to get as specific as possible. Instead of saying "school," they should be specific as to what they are specifically good at. Rather than say just "math," they should break down the skills that they do/are good at in math.

There can be overlap in the columns. For instance, I enjoy reading and I'm good at it. But there can also be things (such as teaching math) that I'm good at but may not enjoy doing. Regarding the last two columns, the students should decide what "paid for" means. Does it just mean money, or are grades a form of currency too?

In the end, the columns should ultimately reflect the following (in addition to other items): school subject matters, hobbies, electives, life skills, character qualities, abilities, etc. Figure 4.1 is a brief example from one of my students.

Figure 4.1 Student Reflection Chart

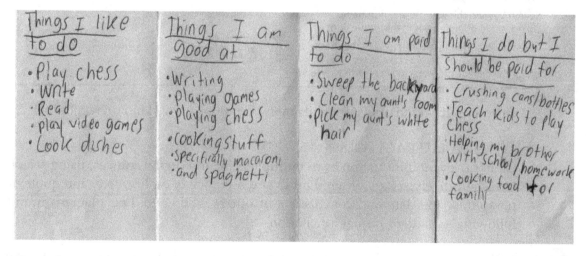

Once the students have this chart to refer to, then they can begin pulling from their lists to pitch themselves for jobs.

2 **Research**: this step is vital because kids simply don't know what's out there to pursue, and jobs morph all the time. However, what the students are looking for in their research aren't simply jobs; they are looking for information on careers. A job is basically something that pays the rent, but a career is a trajectory towards a professional goal. There are many jobs along the way in a career, and the research a child does now will help them learn that key lesson. You have to pay your dues in any profession and jump from stone to stone to get to the place one wants to be.

You aren't necessarily looking to show kids the path to the career in which they will end up, but rather, the goal is to show them tools to continue the research far after they've left your care.

There are many tools out there to use, but I like:

◆ www.cacareerzone.org
◆ https://apstudent.collegeboard.org/home

Both have links that help you think of yourself and your interests in many different ways, and from there, once a student get a whiff of a few careers, they can use what they've learned as a launching pad for other Google Searches and research.

Allow the students to find three careers that might interest them and fill in the chart (Table 4.4) for each one.

Table 4.4 Career Chart

Job Title
What content learned in schools do you need to know to do this job?
What do people do that perform this job?
Why is this career interesting to you?
What do you need to study in college in order to do this job?
Search beyond this website and find three colleges that offer degrees in this profession
Research the offerings at your local high school. What classes do you need to take to set you up for the college program you may wish to attend?

Of course, this kind of research hits many Common Core standards including:

CCSS.ELA-LITERACY.W.8.8
Gather relevant information from multiple print and digital sources, using search terms effectively; assess the credibility and accuracy of each source; and quote or paraphrase the data and conclusions of others while avoiding plagiarism and following a standard format for citation.

3 **Cornell Notes**: you can always have students take Cornell Notes on each of the careers they are researching. See Part II, page 147 for a Cornell Note-taking template.

> **Homework Hint**
>
> Have students keep a growing bibliography of their research. Check this list occasionally to ensure that their opinions are research-based.

4 **Recipe of a job well done**: this is a rather goofy assignment, but it also blends in a multi-genre aspect to the unit. It also allows you to bring in more discussion of the character traits that are necessary to be successful in any job.

Have the students create a recipe that reflects the traits and education needed to do a job (specifically the one they have chosen to focus on). Include both the ingredients and the measurements. The ingredients themselves can reflect both concrete and abstract nouns. See page 89 for a student sample.

5 **Flowchart of pathway through education**: once the students have selected the one career on which they want to focus, introduce them to using a program such as Inspiration. Have the students then create a visual flowchart that is labeled with the steps needed to follow a particular career path. They can create one that might look like Figure 4.2.

Figure 4.2 Sample Flowchart

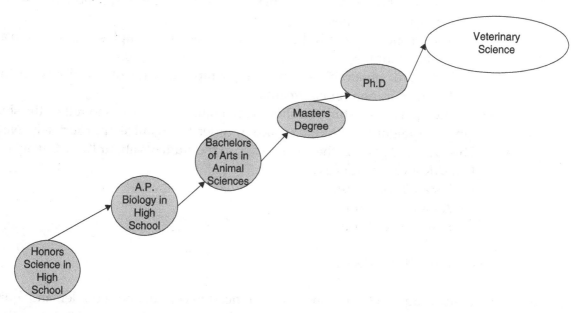

6 **Biography/informational essay**: have students continue researching a particular person who is a leader in the field in which they want to pursue a career. Have them write a biography and/or informational essay on that individual. This is an assignment that can be an ongoing assignment.

7 **"Wanted" journals and business letter format mini-lessons**: throughout an entire week of this unit, have the students conduct some quickwrites that focus on wacky job cover letters. This gives you some kind of structure to teach the actual cover letter/business letter format. Each day, the students walk in to find a different job for which to pitch themselves. They have 15 minutes to construct a cover letter that incorporates what they know about themselves in terms of interests and skills.

So the week might look something like this:

Monday: the students enter and write to the wacky prompt on the board.
  ◆ Mini-lesson: persuasive cover letter format: for this lesson cover the basic visual lay-out of a business letter (see Part II, page 150 for a typical cover letter

outline) and have them convert their journal entry into a formal cover letter using the format you presented.

Tuesday: the students enter and write to the wacky prompt on the board. This time, they must use the cover letter format learned from the prior day.
- ◆ Mini-lesson: persuasive word choice and smooth sentence stems.
- ◆ Follow-up activity: revise Tuesday's post, replacing weaker words with more persuasive choices and weaker transitions with stronger beginnings of sentences.

Wednesday: the students enter and write to the wacky prompt on the board. This time, they must use the cover letter format *and* use persuasive word choice.
- ◆ Mini-lesson: organization of ideas and content: for this lesson, focus on what each paragraph/section of the one-page cover letter should contain.
  - – The first should include the reason why you are writing and what is interesting about the position.
  - – The second paragraph should include concrete examples as to why you are qualified for this position. This is the evidence section.
  - – The third paragraph summarizes, wraps up, and offers to answer any further questions or comments.
- ◆ Follow-up activity: students should annotate their journals to reflect the shuffling that might need to take place in order to organize appropriately. Note: This is a good place in the week to talk to the students about Kelly Gallagher's RADAR revision strategy:
  - – R stands for Revise
  - – A stands for Add
  - – D stands for Delete
  - – And
  - – R stands for Reorder.

According to the Common Core standards, you need to conduct both on demand, quick writing assignments, and those that are permitted to stew and be worked on more thoroughly. Therefore, this assignment hits:

CCSS.ELA-LITERACY.W.8.5
With some guidance and support from peers and adults, develop and strengthen writing as needed by planning, revising, editing, rewriting, or trying a new approach, focusing on how well purpose and audience have been addressed.

Thursday: the students enter and write to the wacky prompt on the board. This time, they must organize their ideas correctly, use great word choice, and use proper formatting.
- ◆ Mini-lesson: voice and audience: talk to the students about the audience that will be reading a cover letter. As wacky as the prompt may be, the students need to take the voice of their letter seriously.
- ◆ Follow-up activity: have the students write two versions of their latest cover letter, one that writes to an informal audience such as a peer and one that

writes to a potential employer. Discuss or journal about the differences in word choice, phrasing, and content.

Friday: the students should select their best, highest-level cover letter of the week. They need to spend time during class revising their letter to incorporate all of the mini-lessons for the week.

8 **Business card**: have students design a business card to hand out to potential employers in their wanted industry. Students can use a program such as the Google Add-on LucidPress or even hand draw the artifact. This is a great time to talk to students about symbols and icons. Perhaps look at different logos for different companies to get inspiration. What does the apple icon for Apple signify and what has is come to represent? Even look at the iTunes app store to look at the symbols each app uses to visually pitch their product.

9 **Bring in an expert**: bring someone into the classroom that hires people for a living, such as an HR person from a business within your area community. Set up norms for being an audience first by generating a list with the students on what listening *looks* like. Have students take notes on questions that are related to the content and skills you have been discussing in class, such as:

- What do you look for in a potential employee?
- What life skills do you want your employees to have?
- Do candidates need to know everything coming into the job or can they learn on the job?
- How much group work and/or collaboration must a person do to be successful in your company?
- How much writing does one do every day?

Have students learn about How to Conduct an Interview (see Part II, page 151) so that they can ask good questions of the guest and use their time with the outside expert in an efficient way.

10 **Interview questions journals**: this is another Monday–Friday quickwrite series of topics. These will be turned into more finalized responses for their oral interviews at the end of the unit. After researching typical questions asked at a job interview, I found that no matter what the job is, the questions are really similar. What that allows students to do, therefore, is predict the questions that they will be asked, and prepare answers for them ahead of time.

Each day of this week should have the students journaling rough draft responses to one or two of these questions. They should respond in QRF (question-response format) for the purposes of encouraging complete, evidence-based answers. See QRF format in Part II, page 152.

If spoken out loud, each QRF paragraph should last approximately 20–30 seconds in oral response. You can time these out with students later. While generally QRF is in informational third person, these should be written in the student's voice, in the first person.

They must answer the following questions:

- Could you please tell me a little about yourself: education, experience, and philosophies?
- What are your strengths?
- What are your weaknesses?
- How well do you work with others?
- What strategies do you use to handle stress and pressure?
- What have you learned from your failures?
- What was a book that you liked?
- Whom do you find the most inspirational?

11 **Resume development:** show students the format of a resume. Find resumes ahead of time that represent different professions, formats, and styles. This is a great chance to speak to them about various strategies of text structures: subheadings, bullets, numbers, bold vs. italics, etc. Remind them that this kind of variety of fonts is meant to be easy on the eyes and to convey the information smoothly and quickly for a busy potential employer. Highlight that more, however, is not always better and that these devices can be overused.

Have them begin to construct a mythical resume, walking them through it step-by-step using different subheadings:

- Experience (most recent at the top)
- Degrees/Awards/Badges
- Education
- Special Skills.

The trick is, however, to only focus on the truth. That is, have them refer back to their initial list of skills and qualifications and spin those facts to make them appear like qualified candidates.

The student sample on page 90 is based on the chart that appears earlier in this chapter.

12 **Final draft of cover letter:** have the students select their strongest cover letter from their week of wacky "Wanted" prompts (see #6). They should finalize this piece and include it in their final digital portfolio. See the student sample on page 91. It was based on the following prompt:

Wanted: Pet Sitter

I am going out of town and am in need of a great pet sitter. Must have experience with taking care of creatures, and must show fearlessness in the face of my dear "Slithy." Must be willing to feed and entertain my pet.

Please send your resume and cover letter to the following address:

Dr. Pythonis

2345 E. Jungle Dr.

Los Angeles, CA 91006

13 **Digital portfolio**: this digital portfolio is due at the end of the unit, but it should be something that is developed from the start in an ongoing fashion. Have the students develop a website. It can be developed using anything from Google Sites to Weebly. Each page should reflect an element from the unit:

- Meet the Candidate Short Essay (homepage)
- Resume (menu tab #1)
- Final Cover Letter (menu tab #2)
- Experience (menu tab #3)
- Best Written Work (menu tab #4): this tab can be a written piece from any subject area classroom that the student feels best represents their best quality and their interests.
- Photo Gallery (menu tab #5): including a Photo Gallery page can cue discussions about virtual footprints and what kinds of shots a potential employer would like to see from a potential candidate.

As the students move from assignment to assignment, have them post their final drafts onto their portfolio so that it grows throughout the course of the unit. You can modify it to suit the individual interests of each student or to reflect a particular position for which they are applying.

Additionally, the Common Core standards require that students use technology to publish their writing. This digitial portfolio clearly hits the goal of:

CCSS.ELA-LITERACY.W.8.6
Use technology, including the Internet, to produce and publish writing and present the relationships between information and ideas efficiently as well as to interact and collaborate with others.

14 **Creative commons and respecting other people's work**: online ethics is about respecting other people's work. This lesson can be reinforced by also showing students how they can show respect for their own work. Talk to the students about licensing and how copyright laws are there to protect someone's efforts by disallowing another person to make money from them without permission.

Then, have them go to www.creativecommons.org. Show them the licensing feature and how to put a free license on their own digital portfolios. It's an easy click, cut, and paste process; and students really understand the options that are offered. It's amazing how tight a license the kids will want for their own sites! Figure 4.3 is a picture of the Creative Commons license that my student put on his portfolio to battle anybody who might want to modify or sell his work without permission.

Figure 4.3 Creative Commons License

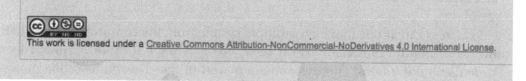

15 **Student-created oral presentation rubric**: each set of students must decide what the five most important points are that they believe the class should be scored on when being interviewed. They are scored on a simple, 1–5 ranking. The end result might look like Table 4.5.

Table 4.5 Oral Presentation Rubric

Volume
Eye contact
Dress for success
Information/content
Fidgeting

16 **Oral presentation**: this might take two to three days. Students are assigned a day on which to apply for a job (aka: present in front of the class). A new job listing is announced the day before each presentation day. In other words, on Monday, you announce that someone is looking for a teenager to test and evaluate new video games. Then, you assign the first group of students that will present the next day. At the end of the first day, announce the next job position and the next group of kids that will be presenting.

On the day of their oral presentation, the students should arrive "dressed for success." Perhaps show the boys a YouTube video of how to tie a tie. Create an atmosphere of professionalism. The goal of the oral presentation is to have the student enter the room, dressed up, with a resume and cover letter in hand. On the projector in the background should be the completed digital portfolio. The format of the presentation is as follows:

- ◆ Step 1. The students should shake hands with the "interviewer." This person can be an outside expert that has been brought in or it can be you, the teacher. It can also be another student, a position that rotates with each student presentation.
- ◆ Step 2. After shaking hands, the student should present his/her portfolio.
- ◆ Step 3. Then, the student should sit in a chair while the potential employer asks one of the questions that the student prepared responses to previously. (See #9 for the QRF responses.) The goal is for students to have their responses also reflect an attempt to align their strengths to the specific position for which they are applying.
- ◆ Step 4. The student must respond, not necessarily with a memorized response, but certainly a previously prepared one. Responses should reflect an attitude of confidence, convincing the employer that the student is a good fit for the job.
- ◆ Step 5. The interviewer scores the oral presentation rubric (or, if it's a peer who is asking the questions, they can fill out a rubric. The teacher, however, should do so as well).

17 **Developing a Career Day for your school**: remember that while this unit is about the interview and employing process, it's also about spreading the word about college and career readiness. The bigger picture is to have your classes host a Career Day for the entire school.

A Career Day is one in which multiple people from the community come to the school and do 20-minute presentations on their jobs and the education required to get there. Students fill out interest surveys and are placed in the classrooms of the presenters that best reflect their interests. Then, students rotate to other classrooms to learn more about other jobs. Picture this as a specially designed minimum day.

While much of what it takes to run an event on a school day should be designed by admin and counselors (adjusted day's schedule, breakfast or lunch provided, school-wide set up, etc.), the fact is that inviting, hosting, and thanking guest speakers could easily fall to the students.

Jobs that the students can do to contribute to the school-wide Career Day:

◆ research businesses in the area
◆ send out surveys to students requesting information on professions among families or friends
◆ write letters to local community members and businesses
◆ host guests when they arrive; greeting them in the parking lots and escorting them to classrooms, delivering water to classrooms after presentations have begun, etc.
◆ write personalized "thank you" follow up letters to each guest the day after the event.

Student Exemplars

Recipe of a Job Well Done

Ingredients: This recipe makes an unlimited amount of servings.

1 quart of Optimism that you can do it
1 package of Ability
2 cups of Effort
½ cup of Grit
4 tablespoons of Connections with someone in the field (because it never hurts)
3 teaspoons of Go-get-ed-ness

Prep Time:
How long you've been alive

Directions:
In a small bowl, sprinkle the tablespoons of Connections with the teaspoons of Go-get-ed-ness.

Meanwhile, in a large skillet, mix together the Optimism, Ability, Effort, and Grit over a low flame.

Add the ingredients in the bowl to the mixture on the stovetop.

Stir frequently and bring your potential to a boil.

Let cool for 10 minutes, but not so long that you lose your Motivation to try.

Serve warm.

Dylan R.

Jefferson Middle School

1372 E Las Tunas Dr.

San Gabriel, CA 91776

EXPERIENCE

2014 – Narrative Writer

2012–2014 – Chess Club

2012–2014 – Chess Teacher

2008–present – Weekly Chef specializing in Italian pastas

2007–present – Hair Maintenance

2006–present – Custodial Staff

2006–present – Professional Recycler

EDUCATION

2012–present – Jefferson Middle School: I specialized in Writing, Reading, Algebra, and Science. I also excelled in P.E. and Speech & Debate

2006–2012 – Roosevelt Elementary: Attendance Award, Handwriting Award, 3rd Place Science Fair '08

SKILLS

Google Drive * Photoshop * Oratory Speaking * Advocacy Writing * Narrative Writing * Basketball * Badminton * Chess

*References Available Upon Request

Jefferson Middle School
1372 E Las Tunas Dr.
San Gabriel, CA 91776

11/24/2014

Dr. Pythonis
2345 E. Jungle Dr.
Los Angeles, CA 91006

Dear Dr. Pythonis,

I am writing to apply for the position of Pet Sitter. I find pets of all kinds very interesting, and I enjoy spending my day with animals. In particular, I find snakes a fascinating species. I assume that we are talking about a snake as you used "Slithy" as the nickname for your precious pet. Pets that we love so much are considered the same as family members, and I would treat your pet as my own.

I am particularly qualified for this position. In fact, I take care of a different kind of animal: my baby sister. I feed her and care for her daily while my mother is busy doing other things for work or the family. I also have taken care of my cousin's dog. Now, while I know that snakes are very different from these other mammals, I also know what being responsible looks like.

I noticed your "wanted" ad immediately, and I hope that I can meet you face-to-face in order to prove my enthusiasm and experience. Please feel free to contact me anytime, and I appreciate your consideration.

Sincerely,

Dylan R.

The Grit and Motivation Unit

A unit based on vital academic life skills and persuasive letter writing

Table 5.1 Grit and Motivation Unit Facts

Subjects Integrated	Writing: argument/persuasion, summary
	History: The Battle of Agincourt
	Reading: informational entry, dramatic monologue
	Technology: Google Drive, multimedia resources
Skills Used	Collaboration
	Mentoring
	Student-generated feedback
	Reciprocal teaching
	Creativity
	Communication
Duration	Approximately two weeks
Driving Question	How does "grit" apply to the process of applying to challenging classes?
	How do you motivate yourself towards victory or success?

Overview

Grit. It's the hot word these days. Grit is about determination, trying something without confidence of success, and working through a problem even after failure. Sometimes getting students to apply for more challenging classes can only be sold by other students who have been through the experience before. This two-week PBL unit culminates in a motivational letter to a 7th grader, a letter trying to convince other students to find the grit in themselves.

We see kids with natural grit apply themselves towards the most challenging of classes, but sometimes it takes a little more targeted publicity to help a mainstream student see the need to challenge him- or herself. Therefore, it's vital for students to help pitch the concept of hard work to each other.

I developed this unit in order to try to achieve one of our school goals: to encourage a more diverse demographic to apply for the advanced courses that are offered at our middle school. The admin team and I felt that the best way to begin this process was through reaching out in a more equitable way to our whole school community. As the 8th grade honors teacher, I tour around all of the 7th grade Language Arts classrooms, hoping to get more students to apply to honors for the following year. It occurred to me that perhaps I shouldn't be the one doing the talking. This unit permits the voices of the current students to speak to those in the class below.

The PBL elements that are utilized in this one- to two-week unit are as follows:

◆ entry event
◆ student choice
◆ writing
◆ outside expert
◆ collaborative note-taking
◆ authentic audience.

This quick Project Based Learning unit uses fellow students as an authentic audience. In terms of frontloading, the 8th graders spend the year touching base with the concept of "grit" in general. As we move into this unit, our awareness of "grit" focuses on the concept as it applies to challenging oneself. I fold in their study of Shakespeare by analyzing one of the most persuasive monologues ever written, the Bard's "St. Crispian's Day" speech. The students study different motivational techniques by interacting with a variety of motivational speeches and writings, collaborating in a jigsaw activity via Google Drive that requires them to share notes on the various resources. As a culmination, the honors classes write motivational letters to the 7th grade class, using textual evidence from the resources they studied and personal experiences as a means to encouraging the younger students to apply for honors.

The letters are handed out to the 7th graders who will, as a result, learn the level of expectation for the honors class, and they will, in turn, give feedback to the 8th grader who wrote the letter, focusing on its level of persuasiveness. Thus, reciprocal teaching and vertical collaboration will occur between the 7th grade classes and my 8th grade honors classes.

Step-by-Step Lessons

Table 5.2 Step-by-Step Lesson Organizer

Date Assigned	Assignment	Deadline/How to Submit
	Journal entry: what is "grit?"	
	Journal entry and padlet activity: try something new	
	Todaysmeet/Twitter activity	
	Journal entry: what does it feel like to struggle through a challenge?	
	Henry V analysis	
	Persuasive speeches from movies jigsaw activity	
	Notes on guest speaker	
	Persuasive letter to 7th grader	

1 **Entry event**: students will watch a video that will spark some discussion about the need for people to develop grit. You can find the video of the hardest working mouse here: https://www.youtube.com/watch?v=QM6MNw7i6Ng

The discussion should be guided toward the concept that grit is not only about pushing through failure, but about putting oneself out there for possible disappointment simply because the attempt is valuable.

Homework Hint (Flipped)

Have the students read through a resource at home. The resource is a fascinating list of celebrity rejection letters that only made the recipient work harder toward his/her goal. You can find the resource here: http://news.distractify.com/people/famous-people-rejection-letters/

2 **Journal entry based on homework resource—prompt:** based on the video of the mouse and the celebrity rejection letters, what is your definition of "grit?" Use textual evidence from the resources to prove your point.

Homework Hint (Flipped)

Send students the link for the TED Talks video, Try Something New for 30 Days. Prompt: What is scary about trying something new? Have students select something that they themselves can try that's new.

3 **Padlet activity:** in order to assess students' participation in the flipped homework assignment, take the first five minutes of class and have them enter their new selected activity that they will try for 30 days onto a Padlet link.

Incidentally, Padlet is easy to set up and it's free. Simply go to padlet.com. Set up a wall and send the URL to your class. It's an easy exit card for a quick informal assessment or for taking the temperature of the room.

This challenge can be formally assessed or not. The students can log in their time doing their new activity, or it can just be presented as a vow to try and not a formal, academic assignment.

Show the fantastic Ashton Kutcher speech as he accepts a Teen Choice Award. It can be found here: https://www.youtube.com/watch?v=FNXwKGZHmDc

In it, he describes the three lessons he learned in life. He focuses much of the speech on the fact that "opportunity looks a lot like hard work." Check it out; there's an easy connection here to the concept of grit and persistence.

Go to Todaysmeet.com. Todaysmeet is a safe Twitter-like space that permits students to construct microblogs in the privacy of a closed chat room. It's a great tool to teach summarization because it forces kids to get to the point. Have each student add to the feed with a "tweet" of something they had to work hard to accomplish. Print out the entire feed and hang it from the ceiling of the classroom for an awesome and impressive share on the grit your students have already accomplished.

Homework Hint

Show students a graphic like the one in Figure 5.1:

Figure 5.1 Can't/Can Graphic

Ask them what one has to do to begin crumbling the T and what that feels like inside. Do you like the struggle or is it just miserable? At what point in the T's collapse does misery turn to motivation?

Here are also some further resources on teaching grit that you can use in the classroom to inspire an introductory Quickwrite or perhaps a Flipped Homework assignment. Perhaps they just might be used to recharge your own batteries as you proceed through this unit:

- http://www.creativitypost.com/psychology/why_academic_tenacity_matters
- http://www.edutopia.org/blog/intrinsic-motivation-growth-mindset-writing-amy-conley
- http://larryferlazzo.edublogs.org/2014/09/16/self-control-grit-all-that-stuff/
- http://www.boredpanda.com/dangerous-journey-to-school/

By providing all of these resources and the ones still to come, you are helping students set a standard for their own independent research. You are also hitting a particular Common Core standard:

CCSS.ELA-LITERACY.W.8.9
Draw evidence from literary or informational texts to support analysis, reflection, and research.

④ **Frontloaded question**: when writing a speech or writing a letter, what strategies can be used to make it persuasive? From here, you are going to begin to introduce students to a series of famous persuasive speeches.

The first speech that we looked at, in my class, was Shakespeare's "St. Crispian's Day" speech from Henry V. Now, we had already looked at a couple of monologues and sonnets leading up to this one, so my students were already somewhat agile with the complex language. You might need to spend a little more time on it than I did, or not use this resource all together. Read your students and adjust this unit as applicable.

Say:

As we've been discussing, Shakespeare's words and phrases and even stories have inspired books and movies for hundreds of years. Case in point, Henry V's "St. Crispian's Day Speech". Let's look at it together. Remember where this young king had come from. Remember that his people had little faith in him as a prince, but he displayed his mettle soon after his father's death.

Here we are, on the fields of France, in Agincourt. They are facing well-armored troops who have been sleeping in tents, troops that, according to the chronicler Jean de Wavrin, numbered over 50,000. He writes that "there were 8,000 men-at-arms, 4,000 archers, and 1,500 crossbowmen in the vanguard, with two wings of 600 and 800 mounted men-at-arms," and the main battle having "as many knights, esquires and archers as in the vanguard," with the rearguard containing "all of the rest of the men-at-arms." The Herald of Berry uses somewhat different figures of 4,800 men-at-arms in the first line, 3,000 men in the second line, with two "wings" containing 600 mounted men-at-arms each, and a total of "10,000 men-at-arms," but does not mention a third line.

Approximately 8,000 of the heavily armored French men-at-arms fought on foot, and needed to close the distance to the English army to engage them in hand-to-hand fighting. If they could close the distance, however, they outnumbered the English men-at-arms by more than five-to-one, and the English longbowmen would not be able to shoot into a mêlée without risking hitting their own troops.

There appear to have been thousands of troops in the rearguard, containing servants and commoners whom the French were either unable or unwilling to deploy. Wavrin gives the total French army size as 50,000. He says: "They had plenty of archers and crossbowmen but nobody wanted to let them fire. The reason for this was that the site was so narrow that there was only enough room for the men-at-arms." A different source says that the French did not even deploy 4,000 of the best crossbowmen "on the pretext they had no need of their help."

The English were feeling low. They were certain of defeat. But then their young king stood before them and motivated them to battle. The speech was immortalized by Shakespeare who wrote his version of what could have been said that day. It has become a bible, a guide, for many motivational speeches to come.

After showing the students the monologue, spend time analyzing the Henry V "St. Crispian's Day" speech for its persuasive techniques. Students then create a dual entry journal that asks them to pull quotes from the speech and then analyze what is persuasive about that particular line. This lasts two days.

5 **Create collaborative groupings of four students per table**: this is a variation of a jigsaw activity where each student will become an expert in a particular persuasive speech inspired by Shakespeare's monologue from Henry V, and then inform the rest of their group about their findings. Each student will be asked to view a different speech, then take notes via Google Drive to be shared with everyone in the group. This should also take about two days.
Say:

Don't believe that Henry V's speech has inspired writers, even in today's mediums? Check out these links for proof of Shakespeare's influence. Some pay homage to Shakespeare's speech; some might even be called rip-offs!

- Student # 1 will watch Charlie Chaplin's final speech from The Great Dictator
- Student #2 will watch Jake's "This Is Our Land" speech from Avatar
- Student #3 will watch the "Freedom" speech from Braveheart
- Student #4 will watch Aragorn's speech at the Black Gate from Return of the King

Each student will then write an informational paragraph summarizing the speech they viewed. However, they will not stop at summarization. They will also provide an analysis of the strategies used to persuade the speakers' audience.

They will write these analyses via Google Drive and then share their writings with the other students in their group. Therefore, while each student only watched one video, every student will have notes on all the videos as well.

For the culminating writing assignment, students may cite from a peer's notes to help seed evidence in their own letters. However, they then must include their peer's notes in their final bibliography using proper MLA format. Have students use the following address to independently find how to cite notes using this format: https://owl.english. purdue.edu/owl/

Of course, using the Internet isn't just about publishing final results; it's also about collaboration. The activity above hits the following standard for technology-based collaboration:

CCSS.ELA-LITERACY.W.8.6
Use technology, including the Internet, to produce and publish writing and present the relationships between information and ideas efficiently as well as to interact and collaborate with others.

6 **An outside expert is Skyped into the classroom**: after reviewing the Norms for Video Conferencing (see Part II, page 154) a motivational speaker will be Skyped into the classroom to discuss motivational strategies. Students can ask how they can leverage persuasion into convincing a student to show grit by applying to the honors classes. A website to look at for possible speakers would be: http://premierespeakers.com/

Of course, the best way to find guest speakers is to draw on the resources in the room. Distribute a survey to your room parents or even send it out to your staff for help in finding those who have expertise in fields that you need.

7 **Write the motivational letter to a 7th grader** using the resources and lessons we have covered in class as textual evidence for your correspondence.
Say:

Once we have analyzed Shakespeare's speech, it is up to you to motivate others with your stirring words. Imagine that you are standing before a group of 7th graders who are too frightened to try out for Honors English. Perhaps they feel they are not worthy. Perhaps they have never known how to show grit. Perhaps they worry that they won't be able to accomplish the goals of the class. Perhaps they have never challenged themselves before and this is their first time even considering an honors-level class. Write a speech that could inspire others to push themselves harder than they have ever pushed themselves before. Put that speech in letter format and address it to an anonymous 7th grader.

These letters will then get distributed to the 7th grade class.

8 **Seventh graders respond to the letters**: the 7th graders will be asked to write on the letters, interact with them, letting the 8th graders know whether they were convinced to apply for the honors program.

9 **Letters will be returned to the 8th graders with feedback.** See pages 99–103.

Student Exemplars

Figure 5.2a and 5.2b Letter to 7th Grader

Dear Seventh Grader,

I cannot begin to tell you how much it is worth joining Honors English in eighth grade. Though you may not think so at first, keep in mind what the teacher is teaching you and you'll realize how easy it is to understand. People think that "honors" classes are so much harder than mainstream, but that isn't true. Sure, honors classes have more work than mainstream, only because you learn beyond the book, and that the teacher believes that you are capable of the work. I used to think that I was never going to sleep in eighth grade, for I have both honors English and history, but was surprised to see that the work they give you is not as hard as I expected. Many students say, "Nah, I won't try for honors classes. I'm not going to make it," but why not grasp that opportunity? Instead say, "Sure, I'll give it a shot. If I don't make it, at least I'll know that I tried. If I do, then I'll try to exceed what I thought was possible for me."

nice phrase

Digging that quote!

School is a place to learn. A place for students to discover their talents and likings, but also a place for students to push beyond what they can see. Honors English is packed with students who are eager to seek further knowledge of this subject. All honors classes, especially Honors English, go beyond the book. While mainstream classes read the textbook and strictly follow the curriculum, we watch videos, read articles, collaborate with other students, etc. Mrs. Wolpert finds current events and connects them to what she is teaching, which deepens your understanding. Many teachers will say, "Try your best," or "Push yourself to your limits," but they rarely say, "Push beyond your limits."

very interesting

intresting

very hooking

I agree. I like this.

No one is perfect. Everyone makes errors. Honors English expands your viewpoint and encourages you to see situations in a different light. What you thought was wrong may not be wrong, and what you thought was right may not be right. This class pushes students to think in from the perspective of both choices, and understand the reasons as to why one would choose a side.

Love the explination.

"But he'll remember, with advantages. What feats he did that day. This story shall the good man teach his son." This quote is from a speech in which a leader arouses the fighting men to continue fighting for the seemingly impossible victory. Though we are not fighting a war in JMS, the core meaning applies to all. This quote means that the students at the top of the class, or even the ones who improved the most, will become obvious to the teacher, and will be remembered. The last sentence states, on a smaller scale, how the most impressive works will be kept, like how the good man remembers, and be used as an example for future students, like how the good man teaches his son of these events.

very extending

Very true I agree

Try. Try for the sake of yourself and your education. You may qualify for this class, you just don't know it yourself yet. Face the homework, even embrace it, for the teachers will always provide the knowledge needed to complete the assignments. After finishing such amounts of work, you will feel the satisfaction of accomplishment, the satisfaction that you have finished and understood the work of an advanced class. If you make the class, put everything you have into Honors English, trust me, you won't regret it.

I won't. I will try. Thanks for the letter. This letter is the tiebreaker.

Well, I would say that your letter wasn't bad. It was really good. I loved how you used discriptive words. One things for sure, it was amazingly well. I really liked the quotes. Maybe I will try for honors english. Thanks for the letter.

Best of luck!

Ryan ████

—This is very convincing. I like the words you use to discribe honors for english. I think I might join.

This was a great letter, and because of the meaningful words and thoughtful phrases, I have been convinced to try out! Thank you for writing this letter, as it has helped me make an important decision.

— Seventh Grader :)

Figure 5.3a and 5.3b Letter to 7th Grader

Dearest seventh grader,

I write to you in the hopes that you will use your talents to the best of your ability. I understand that Honors English try-outs for the eighth grade are just around the corner, and that you may be in doubt. In a changed version of Shakespeare's famous line, I'd bet you're wondering, "To try out, or not to try out?" I can answer that for you. Try out. "Just do it," as Nike's trademark states. You have gifts, and if you never test them out, let alone have confidence in them, there is absolutely no way that you can ever catch a glimpse of your true ability.

I may not know you personally, or even know you at all, but Honors English is probably still something for you to try. Why? Because taking honors-level classes gives you a small appetizer of what high school is going to be like. Chances are, you're not as prepared for high school than you thought you were, so taking a more challenging class will help especially in high school because it is a whole new world. High school is when teachers "stop holding your hand," and Honors English is a great way to transition from gripping to releasing. In reference to the Disney movie, "The Little Mermaid," sixth and seventh grade is the time when you are "under the sea." You have everything, "gadgets and whatchamacallits galore." In a scholastic perspective, you have easy classes, good grades, you're the biggest try-hard and teacher's pet in the world. But after two years of this, Ariel's famous line, "I want more," comes into play. After two years of barely tolerating the boring classes, you need a challenge, in fact, you probably want a challenge. The best way to get that challenge is to take honors English - a whole new world.

I know what you're thinking, because it's exactly what I thought before I tried out. "Why am I doing this? It's just more work on my shoulders, which I really don't need." But the reality is, you do need the work. You need the practice. It is the only way to brace yourself for high school. You're probably used to not trying, used to barely caring, but you've got to change that. You might be too lazy to try out, and I can understand that. But why hurt yourself in the long-run? Honors English is a great way to earn respect and be honored by kids and adults alike. In Shakespeare's monologue, St. Crispian's Day speech, Henry states, "He that outlives this day, and comes safe home, will stand a tip-toe when this day is nam'd." This part of his speech reminds them that their courage to fight will be remembered when they come home successful. I push this onto you. I say, that when you've built up the courage and discipline to try out for honors, you will feel invincible. I say, that when you make it into honors, you'll be the one person above the rest, who will be remembered by many when they are telling their kids to try out. When you make it to honors English it will be known by many and forgotten by few. I know for sure that on the last day of the eighth grade, you will be remembering this letter and thinking, "She was right, I'm ready for anything."

Again, I remind you - Honors English may at first seem difficult, but you will get through it because nothing worth doing is ever easy. There are two main reasons that you should apply to Honors English. The first reason is that you are prepared for high school and the challenges that come with it. Having classes in middle school as challenging as Honors English will help you figure out the time management and commitment it takes to be successful through high school and through life. The second main reason that you should try out for honors English is because you will be revered by many for your effort and will be looked up to by others who want to try out. As Theodore Roosevelt once said, "It's not the size of the dog in the fight, but the size of the fight in the dog." If you are determined to succeed there is nothing that can stop you, not even someone judged to be better. I know you are strong, I know you can do it. "Just do it."

Sincerely,
Ciannah ▓▓▓▓

This is such a great letter. As great as the president speeches.

I love the way you were writing & telling me all the Quotes in 1st paragraph

I like your essay because it is very "quote-heavy" which means the reader will have something to refer/relate to.

I also love your love for Disney. ☺

-I liked the essay since you wrote many quotes for the reader to think about. These will probably convince me to join Honors English in 8th grade. With this letter, you definitely convinced me to look for more challenges along my life. Thank you for convincing me to join Honors next year.

I really have enjoyed reading this letter and after reading it I am seriously thinking about trying out.

-. I really like how your trying to convince me and I am actually wanting to join but Im just alw- ays fear that I might fail but I will try ☺

Figure 5.4a and 5.4b Letter to 7th Grader

Honors English

Hi 7th grader! To start off this letter, I have to admit, being in Honors English is a pretty legit challenge (not to scare you); and just know that there's nothing wrong with being a little scared and feeling hesitation. I remember that day, walking into the cafeteria and getting cold feet. But now, I'm actually glad that I decided to take that step.

Now, you may be wondering: why? Why should I challenge myself? Why should I have to do all this extra work for nothing? Why should I make things harder for myself? Why should I do all of this *plus* jeopardize my good grades (for all you straight A students)? Trust me, these are the exact questions that ran through my head at that time. However, something in my mind pushed me to do it, to just go for it. I felt like I had to push myself, to test my limits and explore "unchartered territory." I know, you're probably going, "It's just trying out for Honors, not the Hunger Games;" but really, I can explain.

What Do I Get From This?

See, in Honors English, not only do you learn English, you also get to explore various topics and research such as how the intelligent brain functions, superheroes and their powers, and I even learned about the demographics on Indonesia. I understand, these might seem like weird and crazy topics to be discussed in English but it makes it easier to learn. Would you prefer to learn out of a boring old textbook on grammar or watch a fun and interactive video on common grammar issues? (I would chose the second option!) And of course, who could forget Shakespeare? Having Shakespeare related activities this year really made things a lot more interesting. (It really gets your "brain juices" flowing) To sum up my point, in Honors English, you may have to up your game, but it's worth it because you can actually enjoy learning (I know, seems impossible, right?).

Why Should I Jeopardize My Grade?

To be honest, this reason was one of the biggest for part of my hesitation to join. I had already tried so hard the last 2 years to keep my grades up; I wondered, would Honors English be the end of my streak? This was seriously one of the biggest things I feared. Through this past year, I have learned that the secret to maintaining a *decent* grade - just keep up with the assignments and PLEASE avoid procrastinating (I learned the hard way). To get a good grade (for the overachievers), you must be creative. Think up ways to spice up your work, add excitement and sparkle to it so that it stands out from all the others. For a heads-up, you'll be learning more about things like text structures and hyperlinks this year, which is one way to brighten your essay up a little. In all honesty, I'm not the most creative person there is and sometimes, it will take time to concoct your wild ideas and get your thoughts onto the screen. (I remember all those late, no-sleep nights and probably will forever.)

Why Should I Challenge Myself?

Next point of interest is: why should I challenge myself? I think that this is really the biggest question in applying for Honors. This is seemingly the breaking point: where people either quit or go on with their personal opinion/answer to this question. This is actually where I began considering and weighing the benefits. I have no personal or direct experience with this, but as you may have heard, everyone knows that it gets harder and harder from high school to possibly college, so why not prepare for it now? Now, you may be going, "Haha college shmollage, why do I care about something happening in 5 years?" Believe me, time really goes by really fast; this may sound cheesy, but I still remember that first day of eighth grade, not knowing what I was bracing myself for. I believe that if you do the hard work now, then the work load and amount of thinking required later won't dawn on you as bad as it might have been. You can think of it as warming up and stretching before running or working out. To add on, thinking harder can stimulate brain waves which can up your IQ and technically, make you smarter (something I learned this year in English). So ask yourself: Why not?

In Conclusion

To sum up, trying out for Honors was one "risk" that I had taken was something I do not regret as of right now. (I do have to admit, I regret it a little when I'm up at 1 in the morning typing away) However, I can wake up in the morning knowing more than I knew before and probably knowing things most people wouldn't even bother to google in their free time. In the darkest times, just think of what you can get out of this. Most of the time, I like to put myself in the future rather than the present just to get myself motivated to continue. For some of you glad to have finally come to the end of this letter, rethink the points and just try out because you will have a lot of surprises coming your way. All I have to say is, give it a shot because you'll never know if you do not.

-Honors 8th Grader

Vanessa ▮▮▮▮

I don't want to be in honors. :)

well written

- your letter was very convincing and I would definatly try out for honors. I can also really relate to how you felt before deciding to try out.

- your letter was very well written and convince me to try out for honors.

. I am not applying because I'm bad at Language Art. But your letter is well writen and very convining.

The Teach Them to Be Teachers Unit

A unit based on the highest level of communication of all … the ability to teach

Table 6.1 Teach Them to Be Teachers Unit Facts

Subjects Integrated	Writing: informational plan, persuasive business letter
	Reading: informational
	Technology: Google Drive, Internet literacy for research, Google forms, Google spreadsheets
	Multiple intelligences vs. learning styles
	All subjects: depending on the topic selected by the student, a particular student might focus on a Science related subject, a History related subject, an Athletic subject, etc.
Skills Used	Creativity
	Communication
	Critical thinking
	Oral presentation
	Independent learning
	Reciprocal teaching
	Peer teaching
Duration	Two weeks–one month
Driving Question	What are the skills needed to teach others?

Overview

In my book, *'Tween Crayons and Curfews: Tips for Middle School Teachers*, I devote an entire chapter to the rationale of why we must teach our students to be master communicators. That is, I make an argument for why we must teach our students to be teachers. I say the following:

> If what Aristotle says is true, that "Teaching is the highest form of understanding," then should not the "Ability to Teach" be our highest form of praise for a student? After all, when we assess students, what are we really asking them to do? We're requiring that they prove content knowledge and the ability to communicate that knowledge. Is that not teaching in its purest form?

Think about the skills a teacher needs to do his or her job. Here's a partial list:

1. communication
2. research skills
3. problem solving
4. setting rigorous expectations
5. giving feedback.

These are the skills of not only a teacher, but of a leader, of a group member, and of a key player; skills that students will use in their own futures. Someone once said that "Teaching is the profession that teaches all the other professions," so why not sow the seed of teaching early on?

The final chapter in this book takes this rationale a step further by providing step-by-step lessons through my Teach the Teacher PBL unit. In it, students are guided to select an activity for which they have some modicum of knowledge and a great deal of passion. It can be a specific topic or even a skill. They must then teach their peers about this interest and pitch it as a possible future elective to an administrator.

This unit incorporates the following PBL elements:

◆ role-play
◆ authentic audience
◆ peer teaching
◆ student-created resources
◆ oral presentation
◆ student choice.

Try this unit, or its scaffolds, to highlight any subject area. The cool thing about this unit is that you can give students as much structure as you want while still giving them choice. Full freedom of topic will certainly earn you some interesting lessons! If you want to focus their topics, however, on historical or scientific subjects, that would allow you some control over content while still granting them choice.

As I say in my previous book,

Students must be taught to teach. They must learn to teach each other, and in so doing, will learn to teach themselves. After all, education's job is not to always be there for the student, but to give them the skills to be their own source of education during their life. What a tragic classroom it would be if the students always remain the pupils.

Step-by-Step Lessons

Table 6.2 Step-by-Step Lesson Organizer

Date Assigned	Assignment	How to Submit
	Finding a topic dual-entry journal	
	Problem statement	
	Bibliography check	
	Google advanced search screen shot	
	Multiple intelligences quiz results	
	Lesson plan	
	Verifying the evidence Google questioning lesson	
	Developing an assessment	
	Student-created rubric due	
	Oral presentation timing sheet	
	Visual for oral presentation	
	Oral presentation	
	Scored quiz results document	
	Persuasive letter to administrator	

1 **Finding a topic**: the whole focus of this unit is student choice, but as we know, without guidance, students can sometimes select topics that are beneath their abilities. So give them some structure in finding their topic; that way, you've at least had them think ahead before committing to something too challenging or too easy.

Have students list three possible topics and create a dual entry journal that explores the pros and cons of each. They might want to think about the "History of . . ." a topic or perhaps a "How to . . ." kind of skill. A template might look like this:

Possible Topic #1

PROS   CONS
- ◆   ◆
- ◆   ◆
- ◆   ◆

Possible Topic #2

PROS   CONS
- ◆   ◆
- ◆   ◆
- ◆   ◆

Possible Topic #3

PROS   CONS
- ◆   ◆
- ◆   ◆
- ◆   ◆

Some fun topics that students have wanted to teach are as follows:

1. How to solve a Rubik's cube
2. The history of the Los Angeles Lakers
3. How to make my Nana's famous enchiladas
4. How to succeed at Guitar Hero
5. The history of skateboarding

2 **Problem statement**: the problem statement is a formal document that is intended to prove a certain level of knowledge in order to pitch the topic to the teacher. If a student selects a high level topic, but hasn't conducted some basic, fundamental research in order to construct a problem statement, then the teacher knows right away that the topic will not work for that student. Conversely, even the silliest of topics can be made more rigorous by first requiring a problem statement be constructed at the top of the unit.

The format of a problem statement is as follows:

- ◆ A student must construct a short two- to three-paragraph informational overview of a topic that they believe they may want to research further.
- ◆ It also includes three to five questions about the topic that can guide future research. The questions can even be used for Google Searches if needed.

The handout to construct a problem statement and a higher-level example can be found on page 155 in Part II of this book. You can see student samples from a Teach the Teacher unit on page 125.

Regardless of the unit in which it is used, constructing a problem statement hits the following Common Core Standards:

CCSS.ELA-LITERACY.W.8.1.A
Introduce claim(s), acknowledge and distinguish the claim(s) from alternate or opposing claims, and organize the reasons and evidence logically.

CCSS.ELA-LITERACY.W.8.1.B
Support claim(s) with logical reasoning and relevant evidence, using accurate, credible sources and demonstrating an understanding of the topic or text.

CCSS.ELA-LITERACY.W.8.7
Conduct short research projects to answer a question (including a self-generated question), drawing on several sources and generating additional related, focused questions that allow for multiple avenues of exploration.

3 **Bibliography check**: the students need to focus on specific and rigorous research, especially if the topic they've selected (and you've approved) is a fluffy one. Therefore, it's important that while the unit itself may be untraditional, the research you require should have a more traditional structure. That's where teaching about bibliographic format comes in. Having said that, I still encourage independent learning by having the students access the resources that help teach them proper MLA or APA format.

The first thing I do is provide students the link to the Purdue Online Writing Lab, and more specifically, to the general guidelines for web-based resources. I point the way to https://owl.english.purdue.edu/owl/resource/560/01, but they then repeatedly access the resource as needed.

I'd be lying if I said that I showed them the proper way to cite major resources when in fact, it's EasyBib that does that. Frankly, it's Google Drive that does it. As an Add-on from Drive, Easy-Bib allows students to plug in key information, and then the program formats it and adds it as a Works Cited page. It's pretty darn cool. As soon as I show them how easy it is, citing work becomes a requirement for every submitted assignment. No excuses when so much is done for you digitally, right?

4 **Teaching Internet literacy skills—how to Use Google Advanced Search**: see page 133 for more on this lesson. This is an easy assignment not only to require but to score.

1. First, have students go to Google Search (the regular homepage) and type in their keywords or questions to begin their research.
2. Have them mark the number of hits that appeared using their method.
3. Show students how to access Google Advanced Search and require them to explore some of its customization features.
4. Have them record the number of hits based on a more detailed Google Advanced Search.
5. Ask them to print out a screenshot of the customized Google Screenshot and mark their initial hit number and revised hit number somewhere on the page.

Voila! Instant credit/no credit assignment.

5 **Teach students about the Six Steps of Being an Internet Detective** (handout available on page 134).

Homework Hint

Bibliography research check: do quick checks of the growing list of resources each student should be gathering on their topic. Grades can be issued based on proper formatting as well as quality of resources. I only permit students to use Wikipedia once on these lists. It gives them a good jumping off place, but shouldn't define their research. No About.com, eHow.com, or Ask.com allowed!

Besides teaching Internet Literacy because it's a logical lesson in efficient research skills, the Common Core Standards also requires it:

CCSS.ELA-LITERACY.W.8.8
Gather relevant information from multiple print and digital sources, using search terms effectively; assess the credibility and accuracy of each source; and quote or paraphrase the data and conclusions of others while avoiding plagiarism and following a standard format for citation.

6 **Study multiple intelligences**: have students learn a bit about the concept of multiple intelligences. This is not so that they can learn about their own, however. It's more to acknowledge that other intelligences exist in the room that they need to understand if they are to successfully teach the teacher and their peers.

Have them go to www.edutopia.org/multiple-intelligences-assessment and take the 24-question quiz to determine their own category. Then, have them click on each of the intelligences listed at the end of their assessment to discover more about what it means to have those strengths and tendencies.

Ask students to brainstorm different activities that might engage a learner that identifies with that category. This list will help students decide on what activity(ies) to ask their class to do during their presentation.

7 **Create a lesson plan**: writing a lesson plan is a lot like writing an informational essay, but it's broken up by different text structures. This assignment asks them to think ahead about their presentation and deconstruct it into different parts to ensure an appropriate level of rigor. The end result should follow the following template:

Name of lesson:

Duration:

Objective: (1–2 sentence goal)

Materials needed:

◆

◆

◆

◆

◆

Step-by-step description of the lesson:

1.

2.

3.

4.

5.

Visuals to be used:

You can see a lesson plan on page 123 at the end of this unit.

8 **Developing questions using Google**, including how to verify the evidence on a website (see lesson on page 146): I remember an article that came out some time ago that posed the thought that Google was really making everyone dumber. I beg to differ. Google just does what we ask it to and no more. Therefore, we have to teach kids to make Google do the work so that we don't have to.

For instance, if we go to Google Search and type in "video games in education" we get something like 1.8 million hits. However, if we type in a more targeted and specific question such as, "How do teachers use video games to teach middle school American History?" you will find about 10 hits, with the majority catering exactly to the topic desired.

To help students ask better questions, make sure you are speaking the language of Costa's Levels of Questioning in the classroom and the 3 Levels of Questioning (see #9 below for more on this topic). Additionally, teach them to develop questions that incorporate important keywords by having them first use Wikipedia. Yep, I said it: Wikipedia.

Wikipedia is not evil. In fact, many researchers will tell you that it's a jumping-off place for them. I'd say that 80 percent of Wikipedia is really helpful while 20 percent is questionable or biased. The key is to teach kids how to tell the difference.

Incidentally, being able to distinguish between reliable information and unreliable information is a Common Core standard:

CCSS.ELA-LITERACY.W.8.8
Gather relevant information from multiple print and digital sources, using search terms effectively; assess the credibility and accuracy of each source; and quote or paraphrase the data and conclusions of others while avoiding plagiarism and following a standard format for citation.

One of the ways I do this is to have students do what I call, "triangulating the data." That is, they verify the information they've found. (See the handout on page 146.)

Basically, the assignment asks students to read a Wikipedia entry of the teacher's choice. Then, from there, they must highlight main keywords, dates, and proper nouns. Finally, they construct those keywords and vital info into questions that they then enter into Google. The challenge is to ask the right question so that the number of valuable hits that comes up is of a higher proportion than the hits that don't help one's research. Make it a contest. Who can develop the most successful question that brings the perfect website closest to the top of the first hits page?

9 **Creating a quiz**: each student for the Teach the Teacher unit not only presents in front of the class, but also assesses his or her peers for understanding. The time spent on teaching students how to create assessments is worth it. After all, designing their own tests based on their own content area allows you to see what they know as they develop questions themselves. It also teaches them the art of high-level questioning and allows students to see an assessment through a teacher's lens, thus, building up their ability to take future assessments. But you have to scaffold the process for them.

Talk about the levels of questioning. In my book, *'Tween Crayons and Curfews: Tips for Middle School Teachers*, I begin teaching Levels of Questioning as follows:

To begin with, I always reiterate with my students that their brain is a muscle, and like any muscle, it needs to be worked out to stay fit. School, I explain, is our gym.

"Now," I say, "If I lift a 2lb. weight, will my muscle grow quickly and with tons of strength?" At this point I generally reach for a minor barbell on hand for just such an occasion.

The catcalls typically answer me with such phrases as, "No way!" and "Weak!"

"OK, but what if I work out my muscle with a 25lb. weight?" I reach for a bigger barbell under my desk for this demonstration. This is generally met with the occasional, "I wanna try!" and "Let me!"

"OK," I continue. "Would you all then agree, that there are activities that work your brain more rigorously then others? And would you also agree that when a brain is worked out hard, it might produce deeper knowledge then it did when it wasn't being challenged so much? And would you further agree that there are even different levels of questions, different qualities of questions that, in fact, also work out your brain better than others?" I then talk to them about showing intelligent confusion . . . as a means to prove just how much we comprehend a topic.

"For that reason," I continue, "we will be looking at the different ways to ask questions, and we'll decide if they are working out our brains just a little bit or working out our brains in a way that makes them sweat."

This is when I tell them about Costa's Levels of Questioning:

◆ **Level I Input**: I start by reciting something. If it's 8th grade, I recite the Preamble or of it's 7th grade, it's Shakespeare's All the World's a Stage.

"Reciting takes a certain level of skill, don't you think?" I ask, flexing my wrists like I'm working them out with the 2lb. barbell. They nod.

"But has it proven that I understand what I'm saying? Would you agree that proving that I get what's coming out of my mouth might work out my brain further?"

◆ **Level II Process**: I then recite my respective piece again, this time with inflection and passion, punching words verbally that are important and using my face and gestures to highlight the meaning of the words.

"Now," I say. "If I were to take apart these phrases and shuffle them around, say, in sentence strips on your desk, and you were to use the words and punctuation and meaning as context clues to put them back in order, wouldn't you say that you were working out your brain more than you did before?" This time I pick up the bigger hand weights. The students start to nod more, some of them moving their arms too, some showing me their biceps, knowing what's coming.

◆ **Level III Output**: "Now let's say I were to ask you the following questions:

'Using textual evidence, could you predict what would have been the message of the Preamble if our forefathers hadn't used the word *perfect* to describe our union? How would the ideal of our country have changed if they had used the word, *acceptable*?'

'Do you agree with Shakespeare that people have seven ages during their lifetime? Why or why not?'

Would you agree that now your brain is starting to sweat just a little?" I then reach under my desk for a 100lb barbell that the class hasn't seen before. Incidentally, I'm a weakling. I can't lift it so well. Never mind, it's always good for a laugh.

Therefore, if students want to create a more challenging assessment, they won't simply focus on recall. They might want to try to ask peers to apply or hypothesize. Give them sentence stems or keywords to get their thoughts going. You can give them something like this:

Level 1: questions that are Level 1 include sentence stems that ask them to recite, define, describe, list, etc.

Level 2: questions that are Level 2 include sentence stems that ask them to infer, compare/contrast, sequence, categorize, etc.

Level 3: questions that are Level 1 included sentence stems that ask them to judge, evaluate, create, hypothesize, predict, etc.

Explain that creating an assessment has to not only assess for understanding, but it must also keep students engaged. Creating a variety of questions helps to keep students on task. Here are some choices of types of questions that students can develop:

1. Rank order questions: "Please rank your knowledge of the following category from 1 to 5, 5 being best"
2. True/False
3. Fill-in-the-blank
4. Matching
5. Open-ended: open-ended questions, like many short answer questions, ask students to apply what they know. These are more authentic but are harder to score
6. Forced choice: forced choice questions actually give more power to the test maker. In other words, the students who are taking the test have no choice but to answer one way or another using only the choices provided by the test creator.

Once you've taught this concept of tiered leveled questions and have taught possible question formats, have the students create a list of questions to assess their own knowledge of their topic. See Part II, page 155 for an activity to help teach assessment creation.

See page 119 for an example of a student-created quiz.

Note: it might also be cool to have the students create the assessment using Google Form so that the responses automatically seed a Google Spreadsheet.

10 **Student-created rubrics**: have the students construct the rubrics that will go on to define their success throughout the unit. That means you'll need them to develop one for their oral presentation as well as one to score the short-answer responses for their student-created assessments.

This can be an individual assignment as well as a small group activity.

First, you have to have the traditional rubric in front of each student. See Figure 6.1 for my district rubric on writing a persuasive essay.

As you can see, it's pretty standards-based and aligned to the same-old, same-old rubrics. It's got all the qualifications of what makes a great persuasive essay . . . except it's boring, and full of teacher-ese. Teacher-ese, while full of academic language, can also translate to blah-blah-blah if it's not easily understood by its intended audience: the students.

Now, starting with the numbers just shown, have the students (whether it's as a whole class, small group, etc.) translate what it means in their own words to get a 5, a 4, a 3, and so on.

I generally only interject my classroom monarch card once when it comes to rubric translation. I insist that the highest score should be described as "Able to Teach This Topic." Let's face it, if every opportunity to learn begins with the phrase "I don't know," then every assessment of having learned should begin with "Let me teach you what I know."

Putting the "Able to Teach This Topic" at the top of an assessment rubric serves two purposes: first, it truly assesses students in their ability to communicate, a skill that is underrated in this era of testing but will be vital to their futures beyond school. Second, it brings a respect for teaching into the classroom, and that's not a bad thing. "Able to Teach" should be the acme of A grades, and by defining the highest grade in a phrase form rather than a letter, students can better understand their goal.

Go through each row of expectations, creating a gradation of accomplishment in their own words. Figure 6.2 shows how my 7th grade fared in its own rubric translation.

See page 122 for an example of an oral presentation rubric created by my 8th grade class for our Teach the Teacher unit. The whole class can design the rubric or each individual student can develop their own rubric using what they wish to be assessed.

It's all about goal setting, being upfront with the students, and giving them ownership of their own learning by teaching them the secrets of teaching as a craft.

11 **Oral presentation timing sheet**: before students get up in front of a classroom to present their lessons, they need to practice, practice, practice. One scaffolded way to help them practice is to have them fill out a timing sheet. The timing sheet helps them assess their own speed and pacing as they speak out loud. Some kids really need to see the numbers in order to believe that they are speeding. That's because the voice in our head sounds perfectly fine, whereas from an audience's point of view, our voices come out differently.

12 **Visual developed**: guide the children to create high-quality visuals to highlight their oral presentations. Remind them that no great teacher would only speak to an audience as a

Figure 6.1 District Writing Rubric

Grade 7

PERSUASIVE COMPOSITION

ELA	Score 5 EXCEEDS	Score 4 MEETS	Score 3 APPROACHING	Score 2 DOES NOT MEET	Score 1 FAR BELOW
Ideas and Development	The response: • States a clear position. • Authoritatively defends position with precise/relevant evidence. • Convincingly addresses the readers' concerns.	The response: • States a general position. • Adequately defends position with relevant evidence. • Generally addresses the readers' concerns.	The response: • Weakly states a position. • Defends position with little or weak evidence. • May not address the readers' concerns.	The response: • May not state a position. • Fails to defend a position with any evidence. • Fails to address the readers' concerns.	Illegible, no response, inaccurate response, or responds in a language other than English
Organization and Focus	• Illustrates a clear, logical organization of ideas. • Maintains a consistent focus. • Clearly addresses all parts of the writing prompt.	• Illustrates a mostly logical organization of ideas. • Maintains a mostly consistent focus. • Adequately addresses the prompt.	• Illustrates some organization of ideas. • Has an inconsistent focus. • Weakly attempts to address the prompt.	• Little or no organization is apparent. • Lacks any type of focus. • Does not address the prompt.	
Word Choice, Sentences and Paragraphs	• Exhibits use of precise, sophisticated & descriptive vocabulary. • Provides a wide and effective variety of sentence types. • Includes highly effective use of transitions. • Demonstrates effective use of multiple paragraph construction.	• Exhibits use of some precise, & descriptive vocabulary. • Provides some variety of sentence types. • Includes generally effective use of transitions. • Demonstrates adequate use of multiple paragraph construction.	• Exhibits use of mostly simplistic (basic and elementary) vocabulary. • Provides a limited variety of sentence types. • May include ineffective or awkward transitions. • Demonstrates weak use of multiple paragraph construction.	• Exhibits consistent use of simplistic (basic & elementary) vocabulary, and/or needless repetition. • Uses mostly short, simple sentences, and/or makes frequent errors in sentence construction. • Does not use transitions. • Demonstrates little of no use of multiple paragraph construction.	
Grammar, Usage, Mechanics and Spelling	• Contains few, if any, errors in the conventions of the English language. • Errors do not impede the understanding of the writing.	• Contains some errors in the conventions of the English language. • Errors do not impede the understanding of the writing.	• Contains numerous errors in the conventions of the English language. • Errors impede the understanding of the writing.	• Contains many serious errors in the conventions of the English language. • Errors seriously impede the understanding of the writing.	

Figure 6.2 Student Created Rubric

ELA	5 – Able to Teach	4 – It gets there	3 – Not Quite, Try Harder	2 – Are you listening?	1 – Epic Fail
Ideas (what thoughts went into it?)	• Great Thesis statement that's a map of the essay • Great evidence, quotes • Great counterargument that says "OK, I get that there are others whom don't agree with my and WHY"	• Great thesis that says what you're going to prove • Good evidence (quotes, personal experience) • Says there are those who don't agree, but don't give them a lot of time to explain why they understand why	• Thesis is there somewhere in intro. • Only some evidence, but not for each point • Only says in one line that there are those disagree (that's not fair)	• What's this paper about? • No evidence (you didn't prove it) • Not one mention of people who disagree	Can't read it, not a persuasive essay
Organization and Focus (can your reader follow it?)	• Really clear, like building blocks from one idea to another • Bull's-eye every time! • Every piece of the prompt is included clearly	• The reader can definitely follow the logic • Generally stays on target • I can find all prompt somewhere	• Um, I think I get where you're going with this • Drifts! • Tries to answer the prompt, but is missing something	• I don't follow you • Blurry, like dirt on your glasses, unfocused • Doesn't answer the prompt	
Word Choice, Paragraphs, Sentences	• Really high-level words! • Tons of sentence types and lengths (texture) • Great transitions (to quote, to commentary, between paragraphs) • Good use of paragraphs to divide ideas	• Good, grade level vocab • Some sentence variety • A few transition words or phrases here and there • Uses multiple paragraphs	• Simple vocab (good, happy, nice, fine, etc...) • Only one kind of sentence/gets boring in the rhythm • Bumpy transitions! • Doesn't seem to understand why you need paragraphs	• Repeats key words over and over • Simple sentences • No transitions (reader must jump across gaps!) • One LOOONNGG paragraph	
Conventions (Do your cross get in the way for your reader?)	• Only a couple of errors (like a really good rough draft)	• Some errors, but they don't get in the way	• Lots of errors but the readers still understand what the author means	• What the heck did the author mean by that?!	

means to convey a lesson. It's about making sure that multiple modalities are tapped and topics are illustrated visually as well as audibly.

There are some basic rules I've put together in a handout for students that can be found in Part II, on page 158. They are meant to help give the children some limitations and guidelines for creating Powerpoints, Keynotes, Google Presentations, and Prezis.

13 **Present an oral presentation of their lesson to the class**: as they determined when they developed their rubrics, Able to Teach is the highest form of proving comprehension. This unit culminates in students role-playing as teachers and instructing a classroom of peers in how to develop a particular skill.

The elements of the presentation must include the following elements:

◆ a combination of different examples of multiple intelligences
◆ a visual of some kind (PowerPoint, poster, video, etc.)
◆ an activity for the students in the classroom (or representatives pulled from the captive audience of peers). For instance, perhaps the class lines up at a free throw line, and after observing the student model how to throw a great free throw, they are given the opportunity, one by one, to try their hand at the task.

14 **Administer the quiz, score it, and analyze the spreadsheet of the responses**: at the end of the lesson, the "teacher" will administer the quiz that the students constructed. If it is created using Google Forms, the responses will automatically seed into a spreadsheet. Otherwise, students should record responses using a program such as Excel. The spreadsheet of results gives students tons of data from which to pull in order to cite evidence for their business letter to their administrator.

Have the students score the assessments by hand for the utmost impact. Sure, they can use something such as Flubaroo or other Add-ons out there, but it's powerful for them to score by hand too. Also, have the students use the student-created writing rubrics to score their short answer responses.

Looking at the spreadsheet can give the children all kinds of insight into what students know and don't know as well as what their peers like and dislike.

One easy way to view specific answers to questions is to use the Conditional Formatting tool under the Format tab on the Menu bar. Here's how to do it:

1. Highlight the column whose responses you want to check.
2. From there, click on Format.
3. Drop down to Conditional Formatting.
4. Enter in the text about which you want information, and pick a highlighting color. For instance, let's say you want to see how many students marked "A" on the third question. You would enter in "A" and then pick a highlight color.
5. Click "Save" and the student should see all of the students who entered "A" because those fields would be the only ones highlighted in that column. You can also specify words as well. This gives a great overview of how students responded.

Using the data that they have analyzed, the students can also create graphs and charts to help someone visualize the end results of their assessment.

Note on scoring and grading: the "teacher" is the one who is getting the equivalent for a quiz grade for the assessment, not those who are actually taking the assessment. True, the student must, as a homework assignment, go home and score the quizzes taken by the class, but this does not count as a quiz for each student, but rather as a participation or class work grade. After all, it is more meant to assess the student as a teacher and to keep the class accountable for behavior and focus during the lesson's presentation.

15 **Persuasive letter to an administrator**: this final component of the Teach the Teacher unit is an authentic assessment wherein the student writes a letter to an administrator to convince him or her that their activity or hobby or whatever should be an elective at the school. See student example on page 126.

In the past, I've gotten different school stakeholders to agree to help in the scoring process as an authentic audience for this final written assessment. The principal, APs, even a couple of Board of Ed members have all chipped in to score a few letters each and to give written feedback based on the student-developed argument-writing rubric. They were instructed to pretend it was a real pitch for the elective, and to respond with great seriousness. In a past book I expanded on this unit as follows:

Sure, it was a mythical program, but many of the administrators actually got really into it, highlighting their feedback on the rubric prior to issuing a score, and even writing comments as to why or why not they would consider the addition of such an elective. Here is a comment written by our principal in response to one such persuasive letter:

"No, sorry Brian. We won't be offering naptime as an elective for next year. I do, however appreciate your research on the sleep needs of the average middle schooler, and I was also very interested in your studies of dream symbolism. Nevertheless, naptime, however necessary, is, unfortunately, not covered in the state standards, and will not be on the master calendar for next year."

Having the students write to other members of the educational community creates not only authenticity, but also a community that extends beyond your classroom. It also lets folks know of the great stuff going on in your own classroom.

In the end, the Teach the Teacher unit is meant to assess students not only on content but also on communication, and it's this very act of being able to communicate content that we should all be striving to assess. After all, when these students leave our year behind, eventually leaving school behind entirely, they must take with them the ability to share, to create, to assess, to problem solve, to research . . . to teach.

Yours is the profession that teaches all others. Prepare them with this in mind, and you will have had a hand in whatever their future holds.

Student Exemplars

Figure 6.3 Student-Created Quiz

1. **Compare and contrast** thermal conductivity and electrical conductivity using the graphic organizer.

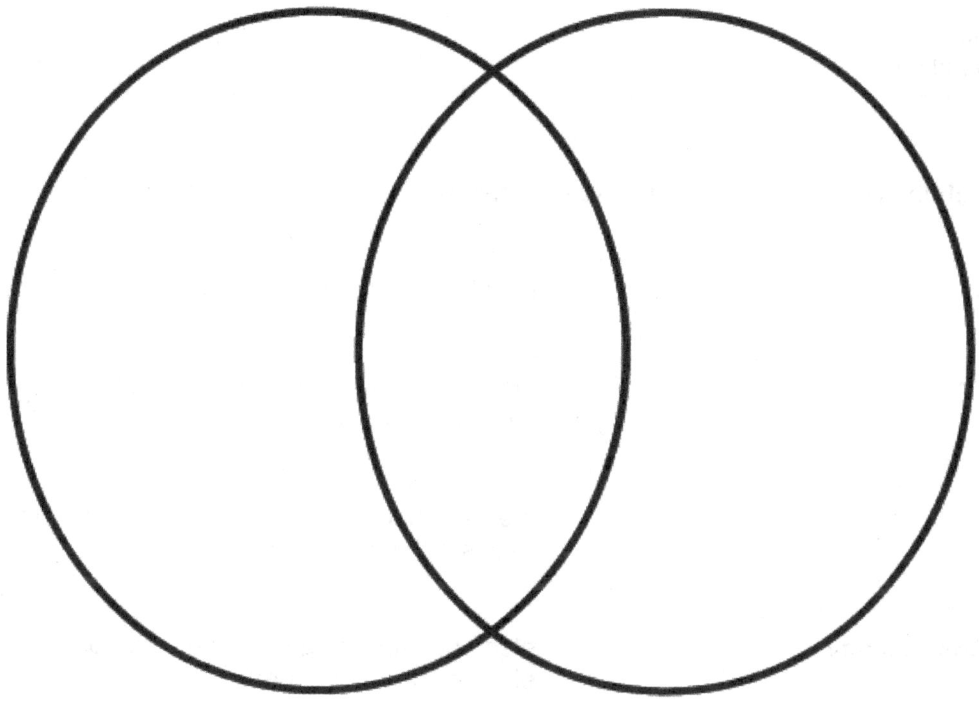

2. **Recall.** Fill in the Blank: Metals are _____ that are good _____ of electric current and _____.

3. **Theorize.** Why do metals tend to decrease as you move from left to right across the periodic table?

_____
_____
_____

(continued on the next page)

Figure 6.3 Continued

4.   **Explain** the reason of corrosion.

_____

_____

5.   **Recall**. What is the meaning of the word "ductile?"
A.   flexible
B.   brittle
C.   unyielding
D.   intractable

6.   **Match** the word and the definition (definitions were found using Quizlet.com)

Metals   the ability of an object to transfer heat

Reactivity   the gradual wearing away of a metal due to
                                    a chemical reaction

Corrosion   the ease and speed with which a substance
                                    reacts with other substances

Thermal Conductivity   elements that are good conductors of
                                    electric current and heat

7.   **Recall.** True or False?
Alkaline earth metals are from Group 1 of the Periodic Table.

_____

8.   **List.** What are at least 10 metals in the Periodic Table of Elements?

9.   **Hypothesize.** What gets fireworks off the ground?

_____

_____

_____

10.   **Create** a question about copper.

_____

_____

Works Cited

"Quizlet." *Quizlet.* Web. 30 Dec. 2014. <http://quizlet.com/>.

Figure 6.4 Student-Created Rubric

Trait	100–90%	89–80%	79–70%	60–60%	What did you think would happen?
Persuasive *pitching yourself *conviction *holds one's interest					
Visual/Model					
Presentation *appearance *posture *nerves (dancing) *eye contact *inflection					
Content *research *length *word choice *applicable					

Figure 6.5 Student-Created Lesson Proposal

Lesson Name: Spreading Germs

Duration: Whole class period

Objective: The objective for this experiment is to see if protecting yourself from germs actually makes a difference from not protecting yourself.

Materials needed:
- ☐ Students
- ☐ Post-it notes
- ☐ A classroom

Step by step description of the lesson:
1. Five minute lecture on how germs spread.
   Visual used: Video on protecting yourself from germs (cartoon for kids)
   http://youtu.be/O5PwLAZNnKc
2. Activity/demo:
   - Everyone will be handed a bunch of post-it notes.
   - Divide the classroom into two groups of people.
   - One half won't be trying to protect or contain the germs.
   - The other half of the class will try to protect and contain the germs.
   - Then the students will just go on with the class period as usual.
   - Whenever a student comes in contact with anything (i.e. a classmate/friend, table, etc.) put a post-it note on it.
   - At the end of the class period, the post-it notes on each side will be counted up.
   - We will see if protecting and containing the disease makes a difference from not protecting and containing the disease.

3. Assessment

Works Cited

"This Is How Germs Spread... It's Sickening!" *This Is How Germs Spread... It's Sickening!* N.p., n.d. Web. 06 Dec. 2014.
<https://www.health.ny.gov/publications/7110/>.

"Infectious Diseases." *Germs: Understand and Protect against Bacteria, Viruses and Infection.* Mayo Clinic Staff, n.d. Web. 06 Dec. 2014.
<http://www.mayoclinic.org/diseases-conditions/infectious-diseases/in-depth/germs/art-20045289>.

"What Are Germs?" *KidsHealth - the Web's Most Visited Site about Children's Health.* Ed. Steven Dowshen. The Nemours Foundation, 01 Jan. 2014. Web. 05 Dec. 2014.
<http://kidshealth.org/kid/talk/qa/germs.html>.

Figure 6.6 Student-Created Lesson Proposal

Obesity has been an issue in the United States for many years. Capable of causing many health issues, obesity affects both adults and children. Obesity can cause many diseases, affecting 34.9% (about seven out of twenty) of adults and 16.9% (approximately one out of five) of children, according to Food Research and Action Center. It can cause Diabetes, High Blood Pressure, Coronary Artery Disease, Coronary Vascular Disease, Heart Attack, stroke, and even cancer, as reported by Arizona State University. Obesity causes excessive cholesterol to build up in one's arteries, therefore clogging blood vessels, and causing strokes or heart attacks. Also, obesity could cause Diabetes. The most common type of diabetes, known as type 2 diabetes, which affects, according to Arizona State University, about ninety to 95 percent of Hispanic Americans, has to do with how there isn't enough insulin (the substance in the human body which neutralizes sugar) to eliminate threatening sugar in the body. This process may lead to coma, or in severe cases, death. To solve this predicament, I propose teach a lesson in how obesity could be prevented, because making students aware of obesity and its capabilities is crucial to ending its reign on our future.

Questions:
1. Why do people become obese?
2. Why do people go from using food as fuel to using it for other purposes?
3. How do people lose weight in a healthy way?
4. How does the weight of our people affect money spent on health?

Figure 6.7 Student-Created Lesson Proposal (Problem Statement)

Problem Statement

People don't train their dogs well, and then they blame their pet for bad behavior. When a household has a guest over, and the owners of the house have a dog that is untrained, the dog will most likely continuously bark and that would be embarrassing. Plus, the dog will scare the guests off. Owners who have dogs like that become very uncomfortable with having visitors invited to their house. As a result, untrained dogs become insecure, act crazy, and tear up things. Because of their poor behavior, the dog will lose a connection with the owners and that family or owner will probably send the dog to an animal shelter. It's like a big circle. With this commonly happening, the rates of dogs in animals shelters will rise and that will lead to a bigger issue. We have to find a way to help people train their dogs or publicize places that offer training. I would like to teach a lesson about how to get a dog to sit, stay, and come. If an owner can just start with those things, it can help guide them to living a happy life with their dogs and to rebuilding that connection between them.

Questions

1. Will an untrained dog still protect it's owner?
2. Will training a dog be easier when they're older or when they're younger?
3. When an untrained dog gets loose, will it run away from it's owner or will it know to stay with them?
4. Can an untrained dog get aggressive towards their owner?

Bibliography

1. "Tag Archives: Trained Dogs vs. Untrained Dogs." *Sanderskennelscom*. N.p., 1 July 2013. Web. 10 Dec. 2014. <http://www.sanderskennels.com/tag/trained-dogs-vs-untrained-dogs>.

2. Deeley, Martin. "How to prevent dog barking." *CesarsWay.com*. N.p., n.d. Web. 10 Dec. 2014. <http://www.cesarsway.com/tips/dogtraining/Dog-Barking-101>.

3. Paul. "Why Training Your Dog Is So Important." *Dog and Puppy Obedience Training and Behavior Problem Solving*. N.p., 11 Sept. 2008. Web. 10 Dec. 2014. <http://trainingunleashed.com/dog-puppy-obedience-training/why-training-your-dog-is-so-important/>.

Figure 6.8 Persuasive Letter to an Administrator

Edward T.
Jefferson Middle School
1372 E. las Tunas Dr.
San Gabriel, CA 91776

Dec. 14, 2014

Dr. Yuen
District Office
408 Junipero Serra Drive
San Gabriel, CA 91776

Dear Dr. Yuen:

Butterflies in your stomach. Heart racing. Naseua. These are the feelings that many people get when called up to present a speech. Whether it's in front of a small group of people or one hundred people, public speaking is one of the greatest phobias in our country today. However, speaking in front of a big audience is an essential skill in life. According to Boundless, 75% of people have a fear of public speaking, and only through daily practice will we fight this fear. For this reason, I firmly believe that Mock Trial should be made an elective.

People have fear as a result of lack of confidence, and mock trial will help eliminate it. In general, as you get up on stage, the hypothalamus, generates the pituitary gland to secrete the hormone ACTH, which then stimulates the Adrenal Glands in your kidneys. As a result, it releases adrenaline through your blood., causing you to be scared. That's why schools are offering classes to help build this trait in students.

Mock Trial is a challenging role-playing competition, where students compete in their county. The competition is an imitation criminal trial, where students are cast as attorneys, witnesses and court officers. They argue a case in front of a real judge and practicing attorneys, who then evaluate how well you did. By participating in this elective, students will, therefore, learn more about our criminal justice law system (and how not to get caught up in it!), build up their self-confidence, develop their analytical abilities, and enhance their ability to collaborate with others, not to mention the real goal: building up their public speaking skills.

Mock Trial also builds up your writing skills through writing direct and cross examinations. Being part of Mock Trial becomes necessary to think deeply about the case in order to draw clear conclusions. It take critical thinking to look through a witness's statement, finding facts where you can use it against the witness, which increases note taking skills.

For these reasons Mock Trial really should be offered as an elective for it helps you develop important skills, and prepares you for when it's your time to make your mark.

Thank you for considering my argument, and please feel free to contact me with any further questions about my research for this activity.

Sincerely,

Edward T.

Part II

Mix and Match Lessons to Design Your Own PBL Units

Bulwer-Lytton Contest Assignment

Overwriting is a common student crime in narrative writing. In an attempt to write well, many students go "over the top." While we don't want to write that way on our assessments, the fact is that one of the ways to learn how *not* to write that way is to try what it feels like to write that way *on purpose*.

According to Wikipedia:

> The Bulwer-Lytton Fiction Contest (BLFC) is a contest that takes place annually and is sponsored by the English Department of San Jose University in Ca. Entrants are invited "to compose the opening sentence to the worst of all possible novels" – that is, deliberately bad. The contest was started in 1982 and is named for English Novelist and playwright Edward George Bulwer-Lytton, author of the much-quoted first line "It was a dark and stormy night." This opening, from his 1830 novel Paul Clifford begins:
>
> "It was a dark and stormy night; the rain fell in torrents, except at occasional intervals, when it was checked by a violent gust of wind which swept up the streets (for it is in London that our scene lies), rattling along the housetops, and fiercely agitating the scanty flame of the lamps that struggled against the darkness."
>
> The first year of the competition attracted just three entries, but it went public the next year, received media attention, and attracted 10,000 entries. Sentences that are notable but not quite bad enough to merit the Grand Prize or a category prize are awarded Dishonorable Mentions.

Welcome to our very own Dark and Stormy Night Contest. Your task is to write the worst hook of all time for any story you wish. The entries must include correct grammar and punctuation despite how overwritten they are. Your entries must be one sentence only, but can utilize punctuation to make it a complex-compound monstrosity. Limit your word count to 40 words or fewer.

Use the Comment feature on this post to submit your terrible hooks.

Good luck, and we all look forward to reading your atrocious entries!

From: Wolpert-Gawron, Heather, *DIY Project Based Learning for ELA and History*, New York: Routledge, © Taylor & Francis 2016.

Hooks for Essays or How to Get a Reader's Attention

Resources: Activities

Getting a Reader's Attention

Project-Based Writing Connection: When adding a written component to your project, use a hook to grab your reader's attention right from the start.

A hook is that first moment of a paper—be it a narrative or an essay—that catches the reader's attention and makes him or her want to read more.

Here is a list of hooks using different strategies to begin the same essay: a piece written about the lost colony of Roanoke. As you can see, there are many ways to hook a reader.

Definition A colony is defined as a group of people who leave their native land to settle in a land with the intent on remaining connected to its original country.	**Onomatopoeia** Scratch. Scritch. The settler quickly etched the mysterious message into the tree never to know if it was going to be seen by another human.
Dialogue "Where are they all?" the first mate whispered, chills covering the sailors as they each thought about the disappearance of the people who should have been there to greet them.	**Simile/Metaphor** When Capt. John White landed back in Roanoke in 1590, he was greeted with a mystery as deep as the sea on which he had sailed.
Fact/Statistic In the late 16th Century, 110 men, women, and children made the brave journey to the New World.	**Staccato Three-Word Lead** Men. Women. Children. They all disappeared without a trace, leaving us to solve the mystery of their whereabouts.
In the Middle of the Action As the ship dropped anchor and the vessel slowly glided to a halt, the men, women, and children all gathered on the deck for a first look at their new home.	**Theme** Traveling to the New World was dangerous, but the people of Roanoke left us a mystery of those dangers that would haunt historians for years to come.

Directions: After reading each of these examples, think of an essay you are working on. You may be revising or just beginning. Try to start the piece of writing using each of these strategies. Then, pass your new list of hooks to your classmate or to an adult family member. Have him or her circle the three he or she feels are the strongest. Pick one of these three hooks to use when writing or revising.

From: Wolpert-Gawron, Heather, *Writing Behind Every Door: Teaching Common Core Writing in the Content Areas*, New York: Routledge, Taylor & Francis 2014.

Narrative Outline

I. Exposition
  A. Hook
  B. Characters
    1. Traits
    2. Inner Conflicts
  C. Setting
  D. Main Story Conflict

II. Rising Action—Climax—Falling Action
  A. Sequential Events (can begin in flashback too)
  B. Sensory Details
    1. See, Smell, Touch, Taste, Hear, Feel
  C. Foreshadowing/Suspense
  D. Figurative Language
    1. Simile
    2. Metaphor
    3. Hyperbole
    4. Onomatopoeia
    5. Etc.
  E. Dialogue
  F. Transitions
  G. Action Verbs

III. Resolution
  A. "Tie it all up"
  B. Lesson Learned, Theme, Moral, Motto

Remember to keep the six traits in mind. You can never write without them close at hand:

◆ sentence variety
◆ voice
◆ word choice
◆ proper conventions
◆ great ideas
◆ easy to follow organization.

From: Wolpert-Gawron, Heather, *DIY Project Based Learning for ELA and History*, New York: Routledge, © Taylor & Francis 2016.

Character Traits Chart

Character name:

Age:

Life motto (theme):

Table 7.1 Character Traits Chart

Physical description	Personality
Goals, objectives, dreams . . .	What others say about this person

Google Advanced Search

Today, we will be looking at Google Advanced Search and doing an activity regarding developing questions as search functions.

- Go to www.google.com.

- Let's say you are researching for an argument essay on games used in education. Type in *video games in school*.

- How many hits do you get? _____

Geesh! That's a lot. Google is asking you to go through how many pages? And I bet not all of them even apply to the topic that you are looking for.

Some say Google makes you dumber; but I say that we have to be smarter to make Google do the work for us.

- Now go to http://www.google.com/advanced_search

- You'll see all kinds of fields that you can customize to make Google do the work for you.

- In the first field, type in a specific question, the most specific you can think of, that is related to the topic.

- In the Language field, select English.

- In the Region field, select United States.

- In the Last Update field, select past month.

- In the usage rights field, select Free to use or share.

- Now, click Advanced Search.

- If you look at the Google menu, you will see a button called Search Tools. Click that.

- Now, how many hits do you have? _____

Six Steps of Being an Internet Detective

Researching Reliably

Being An Internet Detective: The Six Accuracy Steps Handout

ONLINE

The best part of the Internet is also the most suspicious part: the fact that anyone can write anything. The Internet is exciting because you have access to experts and information that your parents and grandparents never had access to. You can take a college level class, you can study any subject you want, and you can find the answers to almost anything. But it also means that anyone can put up a website that is false or misleading, and you don't want to fall for it.

Computers may be fast, but they aren't smart. That's where you come in. You need to check websites for accuracy before you use their information as fact. Here are six steps to check for accuracy:

☐ **Use Your Common Sense**

Ask questions. Asking questions is a sure sign of how smart you are. As you read website content, make sure you always ask yourself the following questions:

- Who is the author of this site?
- Is there evidence to support what the author is saying?
- Is there evidence somewhere that supports or disagrees with this author?
- Is this author biased?

☐ **Verify the Evidence**

Be a detective with everything you read. The answers all lie in the evidence. Keep on the lookout for:

- proper nouns
- dates
- important keywords

Take this embedded information to a search engine (like Google) and find other believable references to back up your information.

☐ **Triangulate the Data**

Look at the word "triangulate." The prefix is "tri-," which means _____. What this means is that if you can't find three sources to back up your fact, then you can't really know for sure if your fact is credible or not. Read suspiciously!

©Teacher Created Resources, Inc.

From: Wolpert-Gawron, Heather, *'Tween Crayons and Curfews: Tips for Middle School Teachers,* New York: Routledge, Taylor & Francis 2013.

Researching Reliably

Being An Internet Detective:
The Six Accuracy Steps Handout *(cont.)*

☐ **Follow the Links**

To where a page links is as important as what information is on that actual page. Click on the external links to find the next layer of information about the author and his or her intent. Perhaps you'll be linked to an encyclopedia entry (reliable link), or perhaps you'll be directed to an Amazon or Café Press product (unreliable link). Don't fall for a website that's really an elaborate ad to sell someone's product or point of view!

☐ **Analyze The URL**

This is by no means foolproof, but it is a place to start in verifying the accuracy of the site.

☐ **Check the Publisher**

If possible, use websites like **easywhois.com** to check the background on the site to help you answer some of the questions in your head.

By checking off your accuracy checklist, you will have diminished the chances that you have fallen for a false website or a website that is more promotional than fact.

Congratulations! You are now an Internet Detective.

From: Wolpert-Gawron, Heather, *'Tween Crayons and Curfews: Tips for Middle School Teachers,* New York: Routledge, Taylor & Francis 2013.

How to Write a Newspaper Article

Some of how we learn to write is by recognizing the components that make up a good document. Print out an article from a website such as https://www.cnn.com/studentnews or https://newsela.com/. It can be on a topic of your own choice.

Annotate your article as follows:

- Circle the Who.

- Put a square around the What.

- Make a squiggly line under the When.

- Make a cloud around the Where.

- Put brackets around the sentences that explain Why or How.

As you write your own newspaper article, remember the following:

- No bias: stick to the facts.

- Pick a stance and be consistent: figure out the point of view and don't deviate from it.

- KISS: keep it simple, silly! Many fun narrative elements such as figurative language are used sparingly in newspaper articles.

The newspaper article that you will be writing must have the following elements:

1. a headline

2. a byline

3. an embedded image with a caption

4. the article itself.

From: Wolpert-Gawron, Heather, *DIY Project Based Learning for ELA and History,* New York: Routledge, © Taylor & Francis 2016.

The Problem Statement

You are going to be developing what is called a "problem statement." In terms of college and career readiness, a problem statement is used anywhere from a doctorate thesis to a business proposal. It states the goal for your research and the problem you wish to solve. Ultimately, it is meant to help focus the topic of your persuasive TED speech.

To create a problem statement, you must write a paragraph that includes the following information:

1. states the broad problem/topic that you are interested in researching
2. defines the problem you will be solving by narrowing the issue
3. describes why it needs to be investigated by giving background information and context
4. states your goals in writing and researching this problem (I will . . ., I plan . . ., I would like . . ., I propose . . ., etc.).

From there, you will develop three to five questions based on the problem statement. These specific questions will further serve to guide your writing. By answering them through your investigation, you should then more easily find a solution or answer to your problem, which will be a main focus of your persuasive speech.

Here is an example of a completed problem statement and five corresponding questions that are specific to our speech-writing assignment. Notice how the paragraph starts out broad in its scope and narrows down to a more specific goal:

Bullying has long been a problem with children and adults alike. While bullying can be seen even in the workplace among adults, those who bully as grown-ups may also be those who bully as children. Children all over our country are victims of bullying, but bullying comes in many forms, some physical and some mental. We must combat this plague from many different angles in order to make bullies uncomfortable in their intimidation. I propose to write an argumentation speech that investigates the different forms of bullying and how we can band together to stop it.

Questions:

1. *What are the forms of bullying?*
2. *What defines bullying?*
3. *Can a bully be reformed?*
4. *What are methods a victim can use to stop being bullied?*
5. *What can schools, the government, laws, families do to invest in solving this problem?*

Writing with Numeracy Lesson

Textual *evidence* can be found in the form of both words and numbers. Sure, we use anecdotal evidence and personal experience as a form of evidence; but those aren't the most convincing because they show *bias*. However, a more solid form of evidence can be found in numerical data. Throughout this unit, you will be expected to provide proof of your findings in evidence presented in writing, in *infographics*, and in numbers. *Graphs, stats, and polls* will also play a part in your final submission. All of these methods and more will help convince an audience of the importance of your issue.

When writing with numbers, there are a few rules of thumb. Please note that not every rule here is universally accepted. These are the general rules for many experts:

1. Numbers that start a sentence are in words.
   Ten years ago, the factory was a vibrant community of employees.

   Your example:

2. Spell out double-digit whole numbers that are single words. Use numerals for numbers made up of two words.
   Eventually, twenty students came forward with bullying accusations.
   Eventually, the entire team of 24 came forward with bullying accusations.

   Your example:

3. Always spell out simple fractions and use hyphens with them.
   According to the World Health Organization, one-half of the children in the country have been affected by this disease.

   Your example:

4. Round numbers are usually spelled out.
   People use around fifteen hundred plastic bottles a second, according to Watershed.com.

   Your example:

5. Use numbers when expressing decimals.
   According to the Federal Food and Drug Administration, it would only cost $0.10 per family to provide them with this resource.

   Your example:

6. Decades should be spelled out in words.
   The Seventies marked an entirely different decade than the one that preceded it.

   Your example:

7. Spell out ordinal numbers.
   The first time he spoke in front of an audience, he felt weak in the knees.

   Your example:

8. Use numbers for times (if using am or pm) and for use with dates.
   The earthquake struck at 7 a.m. on March 21, 2010.

   Your example:

9. Do not use "from" or "between" before a hyphenated date range. It's meaningless.
   Use: From 1986 to 1987, the city was struggling to maintain its level of economic growth.
   Don't Use: From 1986–1987, the city was struggling to maintain its level of economic growth.

   Your example:

10. Generally, 0–9 are spelled out. Numbers after 9 are written in numerical form (unless they are single word numbers, i.e., twenty, thirty; see rule #2).
    All three students used their cellphones to access their assignment.
    All 11 students used their cell phones to text their responses to their teachers.

    Your example:

Other resources in writing with numbers:

    http://people.physics.illinois.edu/Celia/Lectures/Numbers.pdf
    http://www.businesswritingblog.com/business_writing/2006/03/rules_on_writin.html
    http://www.une.edu.au/__data/assets/pdf_file/0012/10803/numbers.pdf

Researchable websites for data and statistics that may help your advocacy speech:

    World Health Organization: http://www.who.int/en/
    Journalist's Toolbox: http://www.spjvideo.org/jtb/archive/writing-with-numbers/
    Gapminder (fact-based world view): http://www.gapminder.org/

Found more? Send them to your teacher to add to this growing list of resources!

Collaboration Constitution Assignment

You need to design a contract that all group members will sign. Look at the following websites as you begin to develop your charter. You can use some of the format and language to help you develop your document:

- http://www.lce.com/Team_Charters_What_are_they_and_whats_their_purpose_360-item.html
- http://www.mindtools.com/pages/article/newTMM_95.htm
- http://www.teamhelper.com/sample/TC_GuideSample.pdf

Think about the following as you draft your team charter. You are not limited to these questions and your final document should use multiple text structures to communicate your contract.

1. What will be the roles and/or responsibilities of each member of the team as they relate to the project?
2. How often will you meet outside of school?
3. How will you communicate outside of school (using email, Skype, virtual classroom, phone, etc.)?
4. How much time passes before a reply to a question or comment is considered unacceptable?
5. What script can you develop or sentence stem can you use to tell someone they aren't holding their weight or participating the way they should?
6. What strategies can you develop in order to increase participation from members before coming to the teacher for intervention?
7. What are your deadlines?
8. What are the roles/responsibilities of each member as it relates to running the group? In other words, is there a group leader, recorder, timer, etc.?
9. What are the norms of your meetings?
10. Begin your collaboration constitution with a mission statement. A mission statement is an agreed upon set of goals that you all are setting out to accomplish. For instance:

    The mission of our group, the _____ League, is to collaborate in order to develop the highest _____ we can present. We will use our individual talents to help other, and we will abide by the rules of our constitution in order to accomplish your goals.

11. You will end your group charter with lines to be signed by all members of your team.

Online Ethics and Copyright Activity

As we continue working online, it's important that we become more mindful of using online resources ethically. Read the required pieces and answer the corresponding questions. Please note that from here on in, I will expect that *all* photos and music used in your digital projects be cited properly. This citation can either be compiled at the end of a project, on a page devoted to this purpose, or cited under each and every image as "courtesy of . . ." Got it?

1. Go to Google and type in "define: ethics." Based on the results, in your own words, what is the definition of "ethics?

2. Go to the Learn the Web website at http://www.learnthenet.com/index.php/ flashtest/netiquette.htm. In the left hand menu, you'll see "Test Yourself." Take the test. How did you score on your "netiquette savvy?"

3. Go to the About page on Creative Commons at www.creativecommons.org. In your own words, what is the purpose of this website?

4. Go to Google Advanced Search. Find the drop-down tab that allows you to find free fair-use sites from which to pull images or documents. Using Google Advanced Search, find one free, fair use, image-based website to suggest to another student. What is the URL of this website?

5. Watch the video on the four factors of fair use from the MIT Library. You can find it at http://techtv.mit.edu/videos/4882. What are the four factors we consider when we evaluate for fair use? Please use bullet points to identify these four points.

6. Go to the About page on the Library of Congress copyright website at http:// copyright.gov/about/ Read the page, and summarize the gist of that page in a paragraph (200 words or less).

7. The final piece is a contract of sorts. Type your name below as a signature of understanding of the following statement: *I understand that every image and piece of music must be cited on every project from here on in throughout this school year.*

Understanding Infographics Lesson

1. What is an infographic?
    Look at the following infographic and answer the questions below:
    http://www.customermagnetism.com/infographics/what-is-an-infographic/

    ◆ An infographic is "a data-rich _____ of a thesis."

    ◆ What percent of information transmitted to the brain is visual? _____ percent.

    ◆ What percent of people respond better to visual information than to text? _____ percent.

2. Analyzing an infographic
    Once done, look at the following infographic from Princeton University and answer the questions below:
    http://www.princeton.edu/ ina/infographics/water.html

    Examine it closely, and then analyze the infographic in one to four paragraphs. Remember to cite the graphic specifically as evidence for your analysis. Each of the following questions does not need to be in its own paragraph. Instead, find a way to organize your thoughts so that your short answer essay includes all of the necessary responses.

    ◆ Based on what you know about the components of the word, what does the word "infographic" mean?

    ◆ What is the overarching issue that the infographic describes?

    ◆ An infographic is like an essay, but it uses symbols, images, text, and data to prove and persuade. It is rich with information. What was the most stunning or interesting piece of information that you learned from this graphic?

    ◆ What symbols were used to create this infographic (feel free to bullet your responses)?

    ◆ Looking at text structure, how does the artist highlight a particular topic or draw your attention to a particular element?

    ◆ Who are the sources of this information?

Executive Summary Outline

Imagine you are a busy executive. You don't have time to read a 10-page report on a theory about how to solve a problem. What you need is an executive summary. The purpose of an executive summary is to inform a reader quickly about a complex topic, so the document must be simple and easy to read so that anyone can understand the issue and the proposed solution. An executive summary does the following:

- summarizes the main points of your issue
- analyzes the most important points
- recommends a solution.

A rough outline could be (think of these as sections, not necessarily as paragraphs):

I. Background information
    A. What is the purpose of the report?
    B. What is the scope of the issue?

II. Main points
    A. Major findings/arguments
    B. Concrete evidence
        1. Data
        2. Videos
        3. Infographics
        5. Interviews, polls, surveys
    C. Methods currently used to solve the problem
    D. How to publicize the issue

IV. Final recommendations

Note:

- keep language strong and positive
- no more than 2–3 pages in length
- consider using subtitles, bold, or bullets to help organize your document
- short, readable paragraphs.

Remember to keep the six traits in mind. You can never write without them close at hand: sentence variety, voice, word choice, proper conventions, great ideas, easy to follow organization.

Norms for Backchanneling and Using Twitter

1. Always have the backchannel open in a public place (LCD projector, public monitor, etc.).

2. Have students use their initials or username to identify who said what. For instance:

   ◆ HW: When preparing for a test, make sure the lesson is the last thing you read before bed. (89 characters)

3. Make sure to set expectations for topics of what students can backchannel about. Some basic ways to participate are as follows:

   ◆ questioning something that was said/read
   ◆ relating to something that was said/read
   ◆ comparing a topic with a metaphor or simile
   ◆ predicting where something is heading
   ◆ visualizing a topic
   ◆ evaluating/giving your academic opinion on a topic
   ◆ answering a prompt or question that was posed
   ◆ taking Cornell Notes.

4. Have students practice backchannelling offline first. In other words, have students respond to prompts in 140 characters or less on a piece of paper or post-it. For instance, you can:

   ◆ give them a subject-specific paragraph and have them squeeze a summary down to 140 characters on a piece of paper
   ◆ ask them a content-related question to respond to as an exit card
   ◆ have students develop 140 character questions to ask each other.

5. When students are *not* typing in the backchannel conversation, their monitors should be at a 45-degree angle to show that they are paying attention.

From: Wolpert-Gawron, Heather, *DIY Project Based Learning for ELA and History*, New York: Routledge, © Taylor & Francis 2016.

Internet Literacy: Verifying the Evidence Lesson

Today, we are going to be practicing our research skills. We will be researching the validity of an excerpt from Wikipedia, the scourge of all academic research!

Here is a reminder of where you can find out information about MLA formatting: https://owl.english.purdue.edu/owl/resource/747/08/

Here is where you can have EasyBib help you cite your findings properly: http://www.easybib.com/reference/guide/mla/website

Go to the Wikipedia article on Henry Wadsworth Longfellow (http://en.wikipedia.org/wiki/Henry_Wadsworth_Longfellow). Read the article.

1. In the space below, list 10 keywords or data that are hyperlinked in the passage.

   _____   _____
   _____   _____
   _____   _____
   _____   _____
   _____   _____

2. Select three of the keywords you have listed, and convert each one into a question to type into Google. For instance you might type the following into Google:

   Did Longfellow write "Paul Revere's Ride?"

3. Using MLA format, cite three websites that confirm the information you learned on Wikipedia. Remember, you can have EasyBib do all the formatting work for you! (See link above.)

   Question #1:

   Citation:

   Citation:

   Citation:

   Question #2:

   Citation:

   Citation:

   Citation:

   Question #3:

   Citation:

   Citation:

   Citation:

Cornell Notes

Name:

Course name:

Period:

Date:

Title is a driving, overall question

List of questions	Notes
Summary	

From: Wolpert-Gawron, Heather, *DIY Project Based Learning for ELA and History*, New York: Routledge, © Taylor & Francis 2016.

Literary Analysis Outline

I. **Introduction**

   A. Hook

   B. Background information (TAG: title, author, genre; what you are responding to, who wrote it, what type of text it is)

   C. Thesis statement

II. **Body paragraphs** (Don't ask "How many?" Do enough to get the job done, organizing your ideas into different sections!)

   A. Reasons supporting your thesis (one per paragraph)

   B. Evidence in the form of quotations from the text that illustrate your reasons

   C. Commentary: original thoughts about what each quotation means and how it supports your point (think about connections to self or other media, to the world, etc., and about questions you might have based on the evidence or predictions you can make; perhaps the evidence should be evaluated in some way or visualized in a description)

   D. Graceful transitions

III. **Conclusion**

   A. Thesis statement reiterated and explained

   B. Parting thoughts

From: Wolpert-Gawron, Heather, *DIY Project Based Learning for ELA and History*, New York: Routledge, © Taylor & Francis 2016.

Oral Presentation Rubric

Table 7.2 Oral Presentation Rubric

Volume: can I hear you from the back of the room?	1	2	3	4	5
Emphasis: does your voice sound textured and interesting or is it monotone and flat? How much passion is in your tone?	1	2	3	4	5
Stance/poise: are you rocking and rolling? Are you leaning on anything? Are you fidgeting or are your hands in your pockets?	1	2	3	4	5
Cohesiveness/overall presentation: have you clearly practiced with your visuals and text? Are you "dressed for success" ready to present for an audience? Are you pronouncing all words correctly? Have you put thought into where to stand and where your visuals are?	1	2	3	4	5
Eye contact: have you memorized enough that you aren't trapped into talking to your index cards or to the screen behind you? Are you making connections with your audience?	1	2	3	4	5
Other _____	1	2	3	4	5

From: Wolpert-Gawron, Heather, *DIY Project Based Learning for ELA and History*, New York: Routledge, ©Taylor & Francis 2016.

Cover Letter Outline

Your street
City, State, Zip

Date

Contact's name
Title
Organization name
Street address
City, state, zip

Dear Mr. or Ms. (person's last name only)

Paragraph 1: state immediately the position you are pursuing and how you came to know of the opening. Explain your interest in applying.

Paragraph 2: share your talents, education, and past experience that make you a perfect candidate. Mention classes, activities, paid and unpaid positions that relate. Be specific and strong!

Paragraph 3: give examples that prove you know how to do the job well. Describe the responsibilities as you know them to prove that you've done your research.

Paragraph 4: state that you are available for an interview and would welcome the opportunity to meet them in person. Thank the reader for their consideration.

Sincerely,
Your signature
Your name in print

From: Wolpert-Gawron, Heather, *DIY Project Based Learning for ELA and History*, New York: Routledge, © Taylor & Francis 2016.

How to Conduct an Interview

Tips on how to prepare for an interview:

- Research your topic and the person you plan to interview thoroughly.
- Come prepared with the proper materials (a pen, paper, tablet, and preferably a way to record his or her voice).
- It is a good idea to have a list of questions already at your fingertips. The best questions are those that you can't answer by Googling. You want the subject to respond in a unique way.
- Don't assume they have the time or the desire to meet you. Be polite and *ask* if they would give you some time, and give them an approximate length of time that it will take so that they can plan accordingly.
- Arrive dressed for success.
- Be on time.

Tips on interviewing a subject:

- Use eye contact.
- Ask a question that you've prepared, and *listen* to the response. Then ask a question based on the response that you might not have prepared. Show your subject that you are listening.
- Shake their hand in greeting and when saying goodbye.
- Say "thank you."

Tips on how to wrap up your interview:

- When the interview is over, go somewhere that you can reflect on everything that you remember. Jot down notes on clothes, wall colors, books on their table, etc. Details will help your final presentation.
- Write a thank you letter. Make sure it includes a greeting, a reminder of the interview, a mention of the top few points that were particularly helpful, and end by signing your full name. Remember to use formal, academic language and correct conventions, even if it's in an email!

QRF (Question-Response Format)

Using the correct paragraph structure is really important. If you were building a skyscraper, you wouldn't want the roof stuck in between floors and the basement on top, right? Of course not. There's an order to things that help support your ideas. When we write expository, factual essays, they are made up of a bunch of QRF paragraphs (Question-Response Format.) We use QRF as a standard structure that gets our ideas out in a clear way.

Here is a brief description of a QRF paragraph:

The first sentence is the main topic sentence.

It's beautiful. You can't miss it. It really makes a statement, and it says something about what your paragraph will be about. You might want to take a sentence or two to expand on your main topic.

The next section is the evidence.

This is the proof that your reader needs to believe what you have to say. Your opinion is not enough; you need facts to back up your thoughts. Evidence can be found in quotes from the text, interviews, data, statistics, etc.

The next section is commentary.

Commentary is the original thinking that you add to the evidence. What do you think of it? Does it remind you of anything? Have you ever shared the experience?

The final sentence is the conclusion or transition sentence.

It's like the ground floor of the building. It's where you leave the paragraph behind, walk out onto the street, and into a different topic.

Oral Conference Feedback Sheet

OWN YOUR OWN FEEDBACK!

Ok, so I'm going to sit down with you to give feedback on your essay. During this meeting, you are to take notes to use as a reference later when you are revising or finalizing your paper.

THESIS STATEMENT NOTES: _____

_____

_____

This is great, keep doing it,   To be revised, considered,
don't change a thing!   mulled over, overhauled

Based on the essay in front of me today, my teacher is giving me a (<u>enter grade</u>)
Think about it: Am I satisfied with that? <u>Y / N</u>

Due date of final draft based on our discussion:

Signed: _____   Date: _____

From: Wolpert-Gawron, Heather, *DIY Project Based Learning for ELA and History*, New York: Routledge, © Taylor & Francis 2016.

Norms for Video Conferencing

"Netiquette" is the accepted word for behavior online. It is the expected manners that everyone should use when they are communicating virtually.

There are rules of netiquette that apply to video conferencing at home or at school just as there are rules in the classroom when you are responding to someone's writing or ideas.

1. Treat others with courtesy and respect.
2. Don't use bad language: using bad language just proves you don't know how to say something well.
3. Don't spread rumors or lies: use the Internet to spread information, not instigation.
4. Collaborate and share your expertise: if you have an answer, step up and share. Learn from each other. It's what the Internet is all about.
5. Lurk before you participate: when it comes to video conferencing, listen first to the conversation and know your audience and your setting before choosing your tone or words.
6. Be forgiving: everyone's a newbie at sometime in their life. Everyone misspeaks occasionally or offends someone by accident because they haven't perfected their online voice yet. Let the small things pass, and pick your battles.
7. Don't distract others: if there is a guest online and we are listening to what that person has to say, don't be a distraction in the background.
8. Don't hijack the discussion. Stay on topic.
9. Bring something new to the conversation.
10. Cite your sources with links or other resources. If we are allowing you to backchannel while the guest is speaking, provide resources and links to back up any further information you want to share.

A reminder to those who set up their own accounts; make sure you:

◆ Protect your profile: when you set up, click on the appropriate box to make sure that your information isn't public.
◆ Don't conference anonymously: let people know who is calling.
◆ Ask first, before you call: if you see someone online, send him or her a chat box first with the phrase, "Are you available to video conference?" Don't just call.

Developing a Student-Created Assessment

When you take an assessment, you are proving what you know about a topic. But did you know that developing the assessment itself can also prove what you know about the topic?

To develop an assessment, you need to know the topic, but you also need to know how to ask questions and the types of questions that you can ask. We, the teachers, use a variety of questions to keep students engaged as well as to make sure that different kinds of learners are given the chance to show off what they know.

In the following activity, you will be identifying questions as one of the following: forced choice, rank order, or open-ended. The first one has been done for you:

1. Should the dress code be enforced in school? **Forced choice**
    a. No, it's a silly rule that shouldn't be around anymore.
    b. Yes, if it's a rule, then it should be enforced.

Why did you select your answer? <u>I selected forced choice because there were only two available options I could choose, and both were selected by the test creator</u>.

2. How should the US deal with persons coming from an Ebola zone if they don't show signs of infection? Mark a 1 for the option that you believe is most likely to help the problem. Mark a 5 for the option that is least likely.
    ___ Quarantine them in a hospital or treatment center regardless of their lack of symptoms.
    ___ Test them at the airport based on where they are traveling from.
    ___ Let them return home and put them under house quarantine for 21 days.
    ___ Let them return to their lives unless a symptom occurs.

Why did you select your answer? _____

3. What can we do to save electricity at home? _____
    _____
    _____
    _____

Why did you select your answer? _____
_____
_____

4. What statement best describes your attitude towards homework: _____
    a. It's necessary
    b. It's a waste of time
    c. It helps me learn, but there's too much!
    d. It helps me learn, but I wish I had more practice

Why did you select your answer? _____

Now to apply what you've learned: In the activity below, develop three questions based on your topic of choice. Make one question a Level 1 question. Another should be a Level 2 question. The third should be a Level 3 question.

Feel free to use the following keywords to help design your questions:

◆ Level 1: questions that are Level 1 include sentence stems that ask them to recite, define, describe, list, etc.
◆ Level 2: questions that are Level 2 include sentence stems that ask them to infer, compare/contrast, sequence, categorize, etc.
◆ Level 3: questions that are Level 1 included sentence stems that ask them to judge, evaluate, create, hypothesize, predict, etc.

Final reflection: do you notice a correlation between kinds of questions and levels of questions? If so, what? _____

_____

_____

_____

From: Wolpert-Gawron, Heather, *DIY Project Based Learning for ELA and History*, New York: Routledge, © Taylor & Francis 2016.

How to Annotate Text

We annotate text in order to help learn its contents. But did you know that how you interact with a text is also a great indicator of how deeply you understand that text?

We talk about annotation as interaction because, in a strange way, it creates a relationship between you and what you are reading.

Below is a step-by-step process of reading and annotating your text. These methods will help you tease apart, figure out, decifer, engage with, question, comment on, disagree with, and explore your documents and books.

- ◆ Step 1: Read the text through once for just overall pleasure and understanding. If you don't understand something, just plow on through and you'll loop back to it in your second reading. (It's also possible that you'll get it in your second reading anyway. Sometimes things are just like that.)
- ◆ Step 2: Read it again with the purpose of annotation.

Possible ways to annotate:

- ◆ Put a **?** in the margin next to anything that you think is confusing. Scribble the question beneath it.
- ◆ Put a (★) next to anything you find interesting.
- ◆ Put an **!** next to anything you find surprising.
- ◆ Highlight things you believe will prove important. Watch out for this one, however. Remember that highlighting should be used minimally. Not everything is important.
- ◆ Circle any lines that repeat.
- ◆ Put a (☺) next to something that shows a positive bias.
- ◆ Put a (☹) next to something that shows negative bias.
- ◆ Draw a book in the margins if a passage reminds you of something you read before.
- ◆ Draw a globe in the margin if a passage reminds you of something in the news or around the world.
- ◆ Create a symbol that represents you. Draw that doodle in the margin if a passage reminds you of something in your own life.
- ◆ Write a brief summary at the bottom of your document so you can quickly reflect and refer to the gist of the writing.

Remember that annotating text is like having a conversation with it. Sometimes having a conversation is messy and loud. Your paper and your annotations should reflect that.

From: Wolpert-Gawron, Heather, *DIY Project Based Learning for ELA and History*, New York: Routledge, © Taylor & Francis 2016.

Visual Presentation (PowerPoint) Guidelines

When people give oral presentations, they always highlight their talk with visuals. Visual presentations help to add another layer of information to your material. They also help to engage your audience so that they are focused on you and your topic for a longer period of time.

There are many different ways and many different programs out there to help you create a visual presentation for your oral presentation. PowerPoint, Prezi, Keynote, or Google Presentations are just a few programs that give students access to high quality presentation software.

However, to create a great visual presentation, you can't just copy and paste parts of your essay onto a few slides. There are some rules you can follow that will bump up your level of presentation creation.

1. **Avoid huge blocks of text**: paragraphs are for essays, not presentations. Don't put in your presentation what you plan to say. Your audience can read, after all, and it's a waste of time to make a presentation that really is just your script.

2. **Don't use bullets**: or, at least use them sparingly. Presentations are to add visuals, charts, graphs, pictures, etc., not words. The words should come from your mouth, not the slide. The visual on the screen should highlight what's being said, not cue or substitute what's being said.

3. **Always remember you are on stage**: look at your audience. Use great eye contact, and don't be lured in to look at your own presentation.

4. **Practice, practice, practice**: don't have the first time you are in front of the class be the actual first time you have run-through your presentation. Make sure you have memorized your material and you have practiced enough to know your approximate times. Also, test all technology before your deadline so that you can troubleshoot if necessary.

5. **Use the programs to their best advantage**: if there are animation techniques to help your text or images move, why not use them? Don't rely too heavily on this, however. After all, it's meant to engage your audience and act as a visual highlighter. But your presentation should reflect what you know about using the program; for instance, if you are using Prezi, make sure that you have an image that captures the main idea of your topic as the "bigger picture" image that is made up of all your own slides along the Prezi path. For Keynote, there are tons of things to play with, but make sure you use them sparingly. Don't explode every slide!

6. **Use tons of different kinds of visuals**: there are so many ways you can highlight your main topic or your evidence. You can display charts, graphs, and data. You can have quotes from polling results fly in. You can insert short videos. The list is endless. Don't be trapped to mere text.

7. **Get feedback before your final presentation**: present in front of family. Present in front of friends. Most importantly, present in front of yourself. Record yourself doing your presentation. Watch it and make note of what you want to improve when you are in front of the class.

From: Wolpert-Gawron, Heather, *DIY Project Based Learning for ELA and History*, New York: Routledge, © Taylor & Francis 2016.

Advocacy/Argument Outline

I. Introduction
   A. Hook
   B. Background information
   C. Who is affected by this issue?
   D. Thesis statement
      1. Possible structure: *Opinion + Reason #1 + Reason #2*

II. Body paragraph(s): Reason #1 and Reason #2
   A. Main topic sentence (general statement)
   B. Expands on the main topic sentence (because surely there is more to say on the topic than just one sentence!)
   C. Textual evidence
      1. Quote
      2. Statistic
      3. Data
      4. Personal experience
   D. Commentary/Connection to the evidence
      1. Connect to self, media, world, etc.
      2. Predict
      3. Relate to a metaphor or simile
      4. Question
      5. Visualize/describe in detail
      6. Evaluate/give an opinion
   E. Transition to next paragraph

III. Counterargument
   A. Main topic sentence (states the opposing side's *best* point)
   B. Expands on the point
   C. Textual evidence that includes the strongest case for this side
   D. Commentary/connection
   E. Conclusion that *refutes* this point (i.e. why it's not enough to convince you)

IV. Conclusion
   A. Reiterate thesis (uses different words)
   B. Solution/call to action

Remember to keep the six traits in mind. You can never write without them close at hand: sentence variety, voice, word choice, proper conventions, great ideas, easy to follow organization.

From: Wolpert-Gawron, Heather, *DIY Project Based Learning for ELA and History*, New York: Routledge, © Taylor & Francis 2016.

References

"The 10 Best Superhero Origin Stories of ALL TIME!" *Newsarama.com*. Web. 17 Dec. 2014. <http://www.newsarama.com/15572-the-10-best-superhero-origin-stories-of-all-time.html>.

"10 Painful Rejection Letters to Famous People Proving You Should NEVER Give Up Your Dreams." *Distractify*. 10 Mar. 2014. Web. 20 Dec. 2014. <http://news.distractify.com/people/famous-people-rejection-letters/>.

"16 Fancy Literary Techniques Explained by Disney." *BuzzFeed*. Web. 20 Dec. 2014. <http://www.buzzfeed.com/moerder/fancy-literary-techniques-explained-by-disney#>.

"21st Century Skills Definitions." *21st Century Skills Definitions*. Web. 17 Dec. 2014. <http://www.imls.gov/about/21st_century_skills_list.aspx>.

"25 of the Most Dangerous and Unusual Journeys to School in the World." *Bored Panda RSS*. Web. 20 Dec. 2014. <http://www.boredpanda.com/dangerous-journey-to-school/>.

"AP Students." *AP Courses and Exams for Students*. Web. 20 Dec. 2014. <https://apstudent.collegeboard.org/home>.

"American Film Institute." *American Film Institute*. Web. 18 Dec. 2014. <http://www.afi.com/100years/movies10.aspx>.

"Ashton Kutcher Speech—Teen Choice Awards (HQ)." *YouTube*. YouTube. Web. 20 Dec. 2014. <https://www.youtube.com/watch?v=FNXwKGZHmDc>.

Barry, Barnett. "Why Is Project Based Learning Important?" E-mail interview. 28 June 2014.

Bio.com. A&E Networks Television. Web. 20 Dec. 2014. <http://www.biography.com/people/roger-ebert-554976#awesm=~oAXcwiqPhCwx1G>.

"Book Trailer Video for Matched by Ally Condie." *YouTube*. YouTube. Web. 18 Dec. 2014. <https://www.youtube.com/watch?v=xaeNWL8rlBI>.

"Borrowers' Tiny World Comes Alive In 'Arrietty'" *NPR*. NPR. Web. 20 Dec. 2014. <http://www.npr.org/2012/02/17/147024270/borrowers-tiny-world-comes-alive-in-arrietty>.

"The Bulwer-Lytton Fiction Contest." *The Bulwer-Lytton Fiction Contest*. Web. 20 Dec. 2014. <http://www.bulwer-lytton.com/>.

"California CareerZone." *Announcements RSS*. Web. 20 Dec. 2014. <http://www.cacareerzone.org/>.

"Clockwork Angel Trailer." *YouTube*. YouTube. Web. 20 Dec. 2014. <https://www.youtube.com/watch?v=tntndQF4eV0#t=43>.

Coats, Emma. *Pixar's 22 Rules of Storytelling*. Digital image. N.p., n.d. Web. 22 Dec. 2014. <http://i.imgur.com/DH1lF.jpg>.

"Create Easy Infographics, Reports, Presentations | Piktochart." *Piktochart Infographics*. Web. 20 Dec. 2014. <http://piktochart.com/>.

"Create Beautiful Timelines." *Beautiful Web-based Timeline Software*. Web. 20 Dec. 2014. <http://www.tiki-toki.com/>.

"Creative Commons." *Creative Commons*. Web. 20 Dec. 2014. <http://www.creativecommons.org/>.

"Dipity." *Dipity*. Web. 20 Dec. 2014. <http://www.dipity.com/>.

Dominus, Susan. "In This Dystopia, Teens must Choose Wisely." *The New York Times*. The New York Times, 14 May 2011. Web. 20 Dec. 2014. <http://www.nytimes.com/2011/05/15/books/review/young-adult-books-divergent-by-veronica-roth.html?_r=0>.

"EasyBib: The Free Automatic Bibliography Composer." *EasyBib*. Web. 20 Dec. 2014. <http://easybib.com/>.

Edutopia.org. "Multiple Intelligences Self Assessment." *Edutopia.org*. The George Lucas Educational Foundation, n.d. Web. 22 Dec. 2014. <www.edutopia.org%2Fmultiple-iintelligences-assessment>.

"Employers' Challenge to Educators: Make School Relevant to Students' Lives." *MindShift*. Web. 22 Dec. 2014. <http://blogs.kqed.org/mindshift/2014/06/employers-challenge-to-educators-make-school-relevant-to-students-lives/>.

"Fantastic Characters: Analyzing and Creating Superheroes and Villains." *ReadWriteThink*. Web. 20 Dec. 2014. <http://www.readwritethink.org/resources/resource-print.html?id=30637>.

Gallagher, Kelly. *Write like This: Teaching Real-world Writing through Modeling & Mentor Texts*. Portland, Me.: Stenhouse, 2011. Print.

"Grammar Lessons With Food." *YouTube*. YouTube. Web. 20 Dec. 2014. <https://www.youtube.com/watch?v=Ry-NYbMEbgc&sns=fb>.

"Helvetica—PERIOD." *YouTube*. YouTube. Web. 20 Dec. 2014. <https://www.youtube.com/watch?v=VDLPAE9wLEU>.

"History.org: The Colonial Williamsburg Foundation's Official History and Citizenship Website." *Home Page of History.org : The Colonial Williamsburg Foundation's Official History and Citizenship Site*. Web. 19 Dec. 2014. <http://history.org/>.

"How to Write Origin Stories." *Superhero Nation: How to Write Superhero Novels, Comic Books and Superhero Books*. Web. 20 Dec. 2014. <http://www.superheronation.com/2008/05/29/how-to-write-origin-stories/>.

IMDb. IMDb.com. Web. 19 Dec. 2014. <http://imdb.com/>.

Juliani, Aj. *Inquiry and Innovation in the Classroom: Using 20% Time, Genius Hour, and PBL to Drive Student Success*. London: Routledge, 2014. Print.

"Know This Headline's Font? You're 'Just My Type'" *NPR*. NPR. Web. 20 Dec. 2014. <http://www.npr.org/2011/09/04/140126278/know-this-headlines-font-youre-just-my-type?sc=fb&cc=fp>.

Kyle, Mike. "How Do You Use Project Based Learning?" E-mail interview. 30 June 2014.

"Make Timelines, Share Them on the Web." *Create Timelines, Share Them on the Web*. Web. 20 Dec. 2014. <https://www.timetoast.com/>.

"Marvel.com: The Official Site | Iron Man, Spider-Man, Hulk, X-Men, Wolverine and the Heroes of the Marvel Universe.Comics, News, Movies and Video Games | Marvel.com." *Marvel.com: The Official Site | Iron Man, Spider-Man, Hulk, X-Men, Wolverine and the Heroes of the Marvel Universe.Comics, News, Movies and Video Games | Marvel.com*. Web. 20 Dec. 2014. <http://marvel.com/>.

"Motivational Speaker Speakers Bureau." *Premiere Motivational Speakers Bureau*. Web. 20 Dec. 2014. <http://premierespeakers.com/>.

"Movie Poster: Star in Your Own Movie!" *Movie Poster: Star in Your Own Movie!* Web. 20 Dec. 2014. <http://bighugelabs.com/poster.php>.

"NZ Book Council—Going West." *YouTube*. YouTube. Web. 20 Dec. 2014. <https://www.youtube.com/watch?v=F_jyXJTlrH0#t=75>.

"Need More Time?" *Colonial Williamsburg Vacations, Hotels, Tickets, and Things to Do.* Web. 20 Dec. 2014. <http://www.colonialwilliamsburg.com/>.

"Nurturing Intrinsic Motivation and Growth Mindset in Writing." *Edutopia.* Web. 20 Dec. 2014. <http://www.edutopia.org/blog/intrinsic-motivation-growth-mindset-writing-amy-conley>.

Orphal, David. "Why Is Project Based Learning Important?" Interview. n.d.: n. pg. *Facebook.* Web.

"Padlet Is the Easiest Way to Create and Collaborate in the World." *Padlet.* Web. 20 Dec. 2014. <http://padlet.com/>.

"The Partnership for 21st Century Skills." *The Partnership for 21st Century Skills.* Web. 20 Dec. 2014. <http://www.p21.org/>.

"Preparing America's Students for Success." *Home.* Web. 17 Dec. 2014. <http://www.corestandards.org/>.

Rapold, Nicolas. "Fighting for Movies With Pen and Thumb." *The New York Times.* The New York Times, 28 June 2014. Web. 20 Dec. 2014. <http://www.nytimes.com/2014/06/29/movies/roger-ebert-is-remembered-in-the-documentary-8216life-itself8217.html?_r=0>.

"Reading Literature Makes Us Smarter and Nicer." *Ideas Reading Literature Makes Us Smarter and Nicer Comments.* Web. 20 Dec. 2014. <http://ideas.time.com/2013/06/03/why-we-should-read-literature/print/>.

"Ron Weasley, One of Us." *GeekOut RSS.* Web. 20 Dec. 2014. <http://geekout.blogs.cnn.com/2011/11/04/ron-weasley-one-of-us/>.

"SCENE III. The English Camp." *SCENE III. The English Camp.* Web. 20 Dec. 2014. <http://shakespeare.mit.edu/henryv/henryv.4.3.html>.

"Self-Control, Grit & All That Stuff." *Larry Ferlazzos Websites of the Day.* 16 Sept. 2014. Web. 20 Dec. 2014. <http://larryferlazzo.edublogs.org/2014/09/16/self-control-grit-all-that-stuff/>.

"Siskel & Ebert—Shakespeare in Love (1998)." *YouTube.* YouTube. Web. 20 Dec. 2014. <http://www.youtube.com/watch?v=pVUHF7xLBwk&feature=youtube_gdata_player>.

"Spirited Away Movie Review & Film Summary (2002) | Roger Ebert." *All Content.* Web. 18 Dec. 2014. <http://www.rogerebert.com/reviews/great-movie-spirited-away-2002>.

"'Still Wolf Watching': A SHIVER Trailer by Maggie Stiefvater." *YouTube.* YouTube. Web. 20 Dec. 2014. <https://www.youtube.com/watch?v=QX82ggGCF7c>.

"Superhero Science." *Series.* Web. 20 Dec. 2014. <http://ed.ted.com/series/superhero-science>.

"Taxedo.com." *Taxedo.com.* Web. 20 Dec. 2014. <http://taxedo.com/>.

"Tell Me a Secret by Holly Cupala—Young Adult Book Trailer." *YouTube.* YouTube. Web. 20 Dec. 2014. <https://www.youtube.com/watch?v=HqzUuoAmTJs#t=48>.

"TodaysMeet." —*Give Everyone a Voice.* Web. 20 Dec. 2014. <http://todaysmeet.com/>.

"Try Something New for 30 Days." *Matt Cutts.* Web. 20 Dec. 2014. <http://www.ted.com/talks/matt_cutts_try_something_new_for_30_days>.

"Weebly Is the Easiest Way to Create a Website, Store or Blog." *Weebly.com.* Web. 20 Dec. 2014. <http://weebly.com/>.

"Welcome to the Purdue OWL." *Purdue OWL: APA Formatting and Style Guide.* Web. 20 Dec. 2014. <http://owl.english.purdue.edu/owl/resource/560/01/>.

"Why Academic Tenacity Matters." *The Creativity Post.* Web. 20 Dec. 2014. <http://www.creativitypost.com/psychology/why_academic_tenacity_matters>.

Wolpert-Gawron, Heather. *'Tween Crayons and Curfews: Tips for Middle School Teachers.* Larchmont, NY: Eye On Education, 2011. Print.

Wolpert-Gawron, Heather. *Internet Literacy, Grades 6–8*. Westminster, CA: Teacher Created Resources, 2010. Print.

Wolpert-Gawron, Heather, Eric Migliaccio, and Mark Mason. *Project-based Writing*. N.p.: Teacher Created Resources, 2014. Print.

Wolpert-Gawron, Heather. *Writing Behind Every Door Teaching Common Core Writing in the Content Areas*. New York: Routledge, 2014. Print.

www.wordle.com. N.p., n.d. Web. 22 Dec. 2014. <http://www.wordle.com/>.

"Мышь vs. Печенька." *YouTube*. YouTube. Web. 20 Dec. 2014. <https://www.youtube.com/watch?v=QM6MNw7i6Ng>.